"I loved Bishop Barlow as a semin in ministry. The days we share a Bishop loves Jesus, he loves the nex time he captures his thoughts in wriung, those words are worth reading."
— **Richard Ross, PhD,** *senior professor of student ministry, Southwestern Baptist Theological Seminary*

"Bishop is a driven and passionate young leader who doesn't wait around for permission to help people. He is a benevolent force who carries the light of Jesus into every conversation and interaction. His gospel urgency challenges me to stand firm."
— **Jason Smith,** *Organizational Psychologist/Consultant*

"I met Bishop at my gym in 2016. The first impression I got from him was a humble servant leader for Jesus Christ. He read my book and I can't wait to return the favor!"
— **Anson Walker,** *Physical Trainer*

"When I first met Bishop several years ago, we spent a lot of time talking about Jesus. Jesus is the foundation of our friendship. You will see his passion for Jesus in his writing." Mark Hikes, Bishop's #1 fan.
— **Mark Hikes,** *Author of 15 Minutes with Jesus*

"From the moment I met Bishop, the one word I could think of to describe him is "intentional." He operates with intentionality in every area I've seen in his life! There's a lot to be said for that, especially in a world where we're very self-focused and a generation that seeks approval. He has asked and excepted the call that God has placed on his life and he's operating it fully. We need more young men in the world doing more of that."
— **Kerri Bunn,** *makeup artist, esthetician, and freelance stylist*

"Bishop Barlow is way more than just an author. He has such a heart, passion, and life mission to see that every child around the world has the opportunity to "know" Jesus through His Word by distributing Bibles."
— **Linda Janet,** *Children's Pastor Life Church Walker*

LOOK
IN THE
MIRROR

BISHOP BARLOW

ISBN: 9798302458070

First Edition

Printed in the United States of America

Editor: Lindsay Hendrichs
Book Design: Carroll Moore
Cover Design: Matthew Alford
Cover Photo: Matthew Alford

This book is dedicated to my family.

Thank you for believing in me and
supporting me through my trials. You encouraged me
through this and helped me become who I am today.

CONTENTS

Foreword

I never knew about alopecia until two years ago. I was shocked when I learned that my tall, good-looking teenage nephew was dealing with hair loss. He grew his hair long, able to hide the condition with remaining hair and cool baseball caps. His condition worsened, leading his Dad to share his story. They had been to numerous doctors, hoping – without success – to find a cure. Tyler loves Jesus, and he has a tremendous God-loving family who circle around each other in every fashion. It's awesome to see Tyler mature in his faith as an example to his siblings, peers at church and school, and even to adults. Tyler is an overcomer who is proving to be a wonderful role model for younger kids.

About the time I learned about Tyler's condition, I visited with an intern at our church. He is a jovial guy with a constant smile. In his twenties, I saw Bishop Barlow as a fun-loving guy who loves kids. He also happened to be bald. I had no idea that this was not his choice. Over lunch, I learned that he had been dealing with alopecia since 3rd grade! It was obvious that Bishop was not a victim. He had learned that God had fearfully, wonderfully made him, and that included alopecia. I was inspired to hear about his journey of dealing with this "thorn in the flesh"(2 Corinthians 12:10). Like the Apostle Paul, Bishop had embraced the words of Jesus, "My grace is sufficient for you, for my power is made perfect in weakness" (2 Corinthians 12:9).

During lunch, I shared Tyler's story. Bishop immediately offered to connect with my nephew. Bishop's attitude and willingness to help another brother was heartwarming. I have learned to realize that this is the heart of Bishop Barlow. He loves Jesus, and he is intentional to be a light of hope for others. Bishop and Tyler have talked a few times. My sense is that they are encouraging to each other.

I recently saw a picture of Tyler meeting with an elementary boy dealing with alopecia. It was moving to see this young lad smiling as he shook Tyler's hand on the basketball court. Praise God that there is power made perfect in weakness, and it's being passed along.

Bishop Barlow has a story of inspiration that will encourage those with or without alopecia. We all have thorns. Some are easier to hide. Praise God that He is using men like Bishop to shine in glory for our Savior's sake.

by Alfred Boulden

Chapter 1
Mirror Mirror

"Mirror, mirror on the wall..." This famous quote from *Snow White* never gets old. The mirror is where the Evil Queen seeks her answers; she wants to know who her competition is, who to kill.[1] She wants the mirror to tell her great things about herself, she wants to be the best but senses she may not be, and she looks for affirmation from the mirror. Therefore, she looks into the 'magic' mirror, hoping to find out who her next victim is. Mirrors tell us a lot, especially if we are willing to look with honest eyes.

Who do you see when you look into a mirror? Sometimes looking into a mirror can be a traumatizing experience, while other times, it can make us proud of who we are. Just like in *Snow White*, mirrors don't lie. For example, millions stare at themselves in the mirror in disgust. They stare at an overweight belly hanging over a belt buckle and ask, "How could I let myself get this way?!"

When we look in the mirror, we have two choices: option one, we can turn on our reflection, head down, and walk away sulking; option two, we can walk away motivated. While we may not have that perfect image right now, we can become motivated to do what we can to change. Even though we only see our physical bodies when we look into a mirror, like the 'magic' mirror in *Snow White*, we somehow see into ourselves through mirrors.

I hate looking into the mirror when I know I have sinned. If my anger overcomes me, and I let a few cuss words out, I then hate seeing myself in

---

[1] Shmoop Editorial Team. (2008b, November 11). *Quotes - Mirror, mirror on the wall, who is the fairest of them all?*. Shmoop. https://www.shmoop.com/quotes/mirror-mirror-on-the-wall.html

the mirror because I realize I have messed up. I stare at my reflection in the mirror and ask myself, "What happened? Why did I say that?"

When this happens, I have some choices to make at that moment. I can continue in my shame. I can walk away from the reflection staring back at me, knowing who I saw in the mirror was a big screw-up. I can lift my head towards the heavens and confess my sins to God. Finally, I can see myself in the mirror after I sinned and tell the reflection, "You are forgiven and loved by God. He died for you. You reflect the image of God."

The reflection in the mirror does not define us because it only shows us a moment in time. But it does shine the truth on us in those moments. In my example, I can see either a shameful, filthy-mouthed sinner or a redeemed, repentant, sinner seeking God's grace. Mirrors tell us who we are and leave us with a choice.

When you leave after looking at yourself in the mirror, you almost always turn your back on what you are seeing. That turn means a lot. That turn means you have decided on what to do next. How does that turn from the mirror define you? What course of action do you take next?

I will never forget a defining moment in my life, a moment that I had a long stare in the mirror at myself and was shocked at what I saw. My whole image changed at the age of nine in 2008. Who I saw in the mirror before that moment was a different person, with a different life trajectory. This look in the mirror was almost a door to a different future for me. I don't remember as much about myself before I turned nine. On that day, the nine-year-old boy looking at back me knew there was nothing he could do to change what he saw – no matter how badly he wanted it to. That was when the boy learned that he would never grow another hair on his body. That was when the boy learned that he would be different from other kids, from other teenage boys, from other men. He would be one without eyebrows, without a hair on his head, without even any arm hair. Could this boy in the mirror live like that? Could he be happy while being so…different?

Years later, I have grown to accept my image. I no longer even wish to have hair. I would not change who I am or how I look. I like the way I look because it has helped shape my character. Through this life-altering disease of alopecia, I have grown strength. I have grown inner confidence that doesn't rely on my looks. Ironically, when I had hair and the outer look I thought I desired, I lacked these inner strengths and the confidence I wanted.

Who I Was With Hair

I instantly fell in love with wrestling when my cousin gave me a wrestling action figure. I thought that little plastic man with black tights and a strong, muscular body was one of the best toys I had ever received. My cousin told me that the wrestling figure's name was John Cena. Imagine my excitement to learn that not only was John Cena a wrestling figure, but he was a real person! When I saw what the real John Cena looked like, I thought he was larger than life. I used my wrestling figure to copy all the moves John Cena was doing. I became John Cena's number one fan.

Then, the disappointment set in. I began to collect more wrestling figures and watch more live wrestling matches. As I did, I realized that the first wrestling action figure I received was not John Cena. Instead, it was another wrestler. I was devastated and felt like a fool. (I eventually got the actual John Cena action figure.)

Once a young boy starts watching professional wrestling and playing with action figures, he will beg his parents to buy tickets to the next show near his house. I was no different. Wrestling looked great on the television, but I knew it was no match for sitting amongst the thousands in attendance at a real event. I had to see professional wrestling live.

While my dad lectured me on the difference between wants and needs, he understood my desire to see the wrestlers live because he is also a fan of professional wrestling. It did not take long for me to plead my case as to why he needed to spend money to take me to a wrestling event. I knew my dad wanted to go, too. So, the decision was made quicker than I thought. We decided to go see wrestling live.

Once you go to one wrestling event as a kid, you hope it will not be your last. You anticipate the announcement that professional wrestling is returning to a town near you. Anytime wrestling came close to where we lived in Mississippi, my dad would get on the phone or computer to purchase tickets.

After attending a few shows, we decided to make a big purchase. It was time for us to take our ticket-purchasing power up a notch. No more local Mississippi shows for us. Instead, it was time for my dad to splurge on our next wrestling show. We decided to go to a pay-per-view event in Memphis, TN. Not only that, but a friend and his dad went with us.

The year was 2007, and I was just eight years old, going to my first-ever wrestling pay-per-view event. We left Meridian, MS, and drove to the FedEx Forum in Memphis, TN. That car ride was so surreal. Who cared if I had school the next day? All that mattered was driving as fast as possible to get to Memphis. I was going to be on live television! Most importantly, I would live out a dream with my dad.

As kids, we have moments that we will never forget. For me, this Sunday night in September 2007 was one of those moments. As my dad and I found our seats in the arena and looked onto the ring, I could not help but smile excitedly. The stage entrance was so massive, and the lights were so bright. The wrestling ring looked larger than life. These sights will forever live in my mind, where happy memories are stored.

When the clock struck 7 p.m., I watched as the lights dimmed. Then, finally, it was time for the show to start. I watched a fantastic event for the next two and a half hours. My eight-year-old self was off the charts with excitement. The fireworks were loud, and the slams on the mat could be heard in every seat, above the crowd. But, the most important memory of that night was my genuine excitement and sincere gratitude to my dad for making that night possible. I am not sure what he gave up to buy tickets to the show, but I can guarantee you that he would do it over again. It was worth it.

Fast forward a few years later, and you will still find me reliving that night as I watch it back on demand. I could tell you who won what match, and I could watch it with the same excitement I had back when I was eight. But there was something about that night that was different than it is now. Someone in that crowd was months away from his life being changed forever. Someone in that crowd did not know he had a few months left before his public appearance would never be the same. Someone in that crowd didn't know he would be the cause of questioning stares and lingering looks. That someone, in an arena of over ten thousand people, was me. I had no idea, as none of us do, what was coming for me.

To be fair, I do not know what all the other people in that arena were dealing with. Perhaps they had challenging times ahead, too. Thousands of people came together for one event, each of them with different life stories. My story changed dramatically just months after that glorious wrestling event in Memphis, TN.

Why do I include this Sunday night in September 2007 as part of my story? At one point during that event, the camera showed me sitting on top of my dad's shoulders, holding a sign I made for one of my favorite wrestlers. You can see my dad and me on camera for about three seconds. You can also see one of my last memories of having a full head of hair.

Almost all the time, when someone asks me what I looked like before I lost my hair in 2008, I show them the picture of my dad and me watching wrestling live in Memphis, TN. Not only are people shocked to see me as an eight-year-old, but they are also shocked to see me with straight, dark brown hair. I have come to realize that more people know me as not having hair than as having hair. People know me this way because I have been alive longer without hair than I have with hair. Therefore, not having hair is now part of my identity.

Your Name

In high school, my class and I spent a few days in English class reading *The Crucible*. Each of us were assigned character roles to read. Hearing some of my classmates try to read in their best acting voices was amusing. I think some classmates saw a future in Hollywood while reading their lines in a high school in a small town in Mississippi. This reading could be the shining moment that led to fame and fortune. Others just read the lines with very little energy and enthusiasm. They just wanted to be finished because they saw this assignment as a waste of time.

There is one scene in *The Crucible* that I particularly enjoy. At the end of Arthur Miller's classic, John Proctor, one of the favorites in the town, is willing to sign his name and confess to conspiring with the devil. He signs his name on the confession paper which leads to his freedom, and he avoids death by hanging. However, at the last minute, he cannot hand the document over.

When asked why he cannot hand the signed document to the authorities, Proctor says, "Because it is my name! Because I cannot have another in my life! Because I lie and sign myself to lies! Because I am not worth the dust on the feet of them that hang! How may I live without my name? I have given you my soul; leave me my name!"[2]

John Proctor's quote is powerful and reminds me of the importance of who we are and that our names matter. Our names say a lot about us and our families. I hold my name to a high standard as I want to represent well my family and my great grandfather, the man I was named after. Our names are part of unique identities.

The Bible has special names for those who have given their lives to Christ. John 1:12 says, "Yet to all who did receive him, to those who believed in his name, he gave the right to become children of God." There is a unique two-part message here. To be called "children of God," we need to believe in and receive Jesus as Lord of our lives. Then, we become children of God.

Another example of the Bible telling us who we are is found in 1 Peter 2:9-10. Peter, the author of 1 Peter, a close friend to and disciple of Jesus, tells us, "But you are a chosen people, a royal priesthood, a holy nation, God's special possession, that you may declare the praises of him who called you out of darkness into his wonderful light. Once you were not a people, but now you are the people of God; once you had not received mercy, but now you have received mercy."

Peter says that the children of God are "chosen and royal." I do not know about you, but I am comforted by the fact that the God of the universe cares enough about me, someone who disobeys Him every day, to call me "chosen and royal." This comfort reminds me there is a love greater than my greatest sins.

I believe 1 Peter 2:10 gives us a great illustration of our names before Christ. What were our names before Christ? Our names could be summarized, according to 1 Peter 2:10, as "not a chosen people and without mercy." We were dead in our sins, lacking Jesus's love and forgiveness. We had

---

2 Shmoop Editorial Team. (2008a, November 11). *Quotes - because it is my name!.* Shmoop. https://www.shmoop.com/quotes/because-it-is-my-name.html

no hope of finding mercy on our own. Our name changes, from those who had no future to children of God, took a toll on Jesus, costing Him His life.

The royal king of Heaven humbled Himself enough to be on our level. He became one of us, so we might be called one of His. He paved the way for us to have the most significant name and identity change ever.

Where is your identity? I enjoy my name being Bishop because of the religious jokes that come with it. However, since I surrendered to the call of ministry in 2016, I began to hear things like, "Well, you have a great name for ministry." So, my name and my calling into ministry have led to some funny stories.

One day, my sister and I were in the drive-thru line at Chick-fil-A. As I turned my car around the building to be next in line to pick up our food, I could smell that glorious chicken sandwich and those tasty waffle fries. To top it off, I could not wait to indulge in the delicious sweet tea that Chick-fil-A offers.

As I drove up and approached the employees who had our food, they looked at us with puzzling expressions. One of them said, "Are you an actual Bishop?" I could not help but laugh. I am glad my sister was there to help answer their question. She responded, "No, but he is going to seminary."

Reflecting on the question, "Are you an actual Bishop?" makes me think about how people view our identities and our names. We often view ourselves in different ways in different areas of life. For example, when telling someone about my ministry, Know Ministries, I usually say, "My name is Bishop Barlow, and I am the founder of Know Ministries." In that sentence, I express my name and what I identify with in the moment.

When you are in school, you are identified by your grade. Your sentence could go like this, "My name is Alex, and I am a senior in high school." You expressed your name and what you wanted to identify as. You want people to see you as a senior in high school because that is important to you.

The band Newsong has a song called "I Am a Christian." They also have t-shirts with that phrase printed on the front. (Yep, I have one.) For followers of Jesus, our identities are more than we give ourselves credit for. We used to be rebels against God. Now, we identify as being forgiven. God sees us, His children, as more than sinners. Romans 5:8 tells us this when Paul writes, "But God demonstrates his own love for us in this: While we were still sinners, Christ died for us." We can then proclaim the truth like the song from Newsong, "I am a Christian."

We will still sin. We will still have moments of rebellion against God. We will even try to put ourselves in God's place and take control of situations. However, our focus should not be to take advantage of God's grace by sinning but to embrace and accept His grace when we do. Doing so will remind us of our identities in Christ, children of God forgiven and loved by Jesus, who gives us His grace.

Chapter 2
A Wake Up Call

"Ahhhhh! What is all over my pillow?!" I screamed in fear when I woke up one morning before school, seeing clumps of dark brown hair all over my pillow.

It was my third-grade year. I went to sleep most nights a happy kid, dreaming of the next wrestling event I would go to with my dad. I looked like any normal third grader, short and young with a full head of hair. I washed my hair every day and combed it so it would not be messy. I tried different hairstyles, hoping one would impress the girls in my class. However, one morning, everything in my life changed in one waking moment.

I would never be who I was before I saw hair all over my pillow. Reflecting on this moment that changed everything about me reminds me of facing wake-up calls. Merriam-Webster describes a wake-up call as "something that serves to alert a person to a problem, danger, or need."[3] We all face wake-up calls in different ways.

Some of us face a wake-up call when a spouse boldly proclaims, "Choose me, or I am leaving." Your spouse is giving you an ultimatum, tired of waiting or tired of you choosing something else as top priority. Your spouse has tried to help you overcome an addiction or being away for too many nights only to fail again. It brings your spouse to the final option of laying down the ultimatum no married person wants to hear. What do you do? Do you give up your addiction and struggles that seem to promise you fulfillment and risk losing your spouse and kids forever? Or do you realize that you

[3] Merriam-Webster. (n.d.). *Wake-up call definition & meaning.* Merriam-Webster. https://www.merriam-webster.com/dictionary/wake-up%20call

were given a wake-up call moment and take the necessary actions needed to change to save your relationship with your spouse and children?

A wake-up call can also come in the form of a sport. One day you play a terrible game or have the worst practice you could ever have. For example, you could be like me while practicing tennis one day. As you begin to hit the ball back and forth with your opponent, you realize something is off. None of your forehands or backhands are going over the net. Next, you try to serve the tennis ball to the other side, only to hit it on the racquet's frame and watch as the ball sails high into the sky and over the fence. (Trust me, I have had many of those moments.)

Your coach notices something is off and realizes it is time to pull you aside. "What is going on with you today?" your coach asks in confusion. You have no response as to what is happening to your tennis game. Your coach then looks into your eyes and says, "Playing like this will cost this team the State Championship." As you watch your coach walk away, you drop your head, trying to block out all the surrounding distractions so you can process those words from your coach. Those words can be a wake-up call to you to change something quickly or risk a loss for your team.

One final example of a wake-up call should be familiar to many students. Prom is right around the corner, and you cannot wait for 'the night of your life.' You have a nice car ready to pick up that special someone you finally mustered the courage to ask to go with you. You have your outfit ready and realize nothing can stop you from having a grand time except your grades.

Your parents have been on you for weeks, telling you that your grades must improve. However, they do not realize the importance of hanging out late at night with friends and that hours spent on a PlayStation or Xbox are more important than studying. You may think, "Why can't parents realize that these are necessities in life?"

Any excuse you bring to your parents' attention will not cut it with them. They look at you with what must be one of their top three serious faces. Finally, they say, "You have a choice! You either pull up your grades by making an A on the next test, or you are not going to that prom, and that is final!" Luckily for me, I have never heard those words before, but I know my sister has heard similar.

Even though I cannot relate to the ultimatum regarding grades or prom, I can relate to having a wake-up call. The moment I saw pieces of my dark brown hair scattered on my pillow when I was nine years old was a big wake-up call. I sprang out of bed and rushed to the nearest bathroom to look in a mirror to see what was happening and how noticeable my hair loss was. Though I only saw it in that moment, this part of my story actually started six weeks before this dreadful moment.

104 Degree Fever

One day, as I talked with a friend's parent about fevers, I suddenly made a connection and said, "The day after my ninth birthday, I got sick, and I had a 104-degree fever." I watched as this parent had a wave of shock over her face. "That is dangerous," she informed me. I knew I was sick when I had a 104-degree fever, but I never considered the dangers of it. Six degrees above normal, a 104-degree fever can lead to severe problems.

After I turned nine years old, I had the worst week of sickness in my life. I could not keep any medicine down and had zero strength to get off the couch. Usually, when I miss a few days of school, my mind enters panic mode as I think about the notes I need to make up and the assignments I need to complete. But that week, as I lay on the couch, feeling like death, I didn't care about what test I missed or what homework assignment I needed to complete before returning to school.

My mom nursed me the best she could. She drove to the pharmacy to pick up my medicine and brought me cold rags to place over my head. She cooked me the classic sick patient food, chicken noodle soup. As much as she tried, nothing worked. I threw up every time I took my medicine or ate food. As I tell this story, I ask myself, "Was this week my near-death experience?"

My sickness got so bad that I kept one of my mom's good kitchen pots next to the couch I laid on for a week. I kept that pot near me because I knew it was only a matter of time before whatever I ate or drank would tell me it was time to return to where it came from. I went from hot to cold in a matter of seconds. One minute I yelled, "Someone give me a blanket," then, "Someone turn down the dang heat in this house."

I continued to lay in utter agony as my mom checked my temperature. I watched as her emotional state was nothing but sadness, knowing her second child was very sick. At one point, she took my temperature, and the thermometer read 104 degrees. That reading potentially played a significant role in my future appearance.

I hope you never relate to the week I had. Unfortunately, some people I know have had it worse than me. If you have not, be thankful because what I experienced after my ninth birthday was horrendous. Feeling this way made me want to get well because I was so tired of being sick, laying on the couch, and missing my friends.

Determination to Get Well

At least one person in Mississippi can relate to what I am about to say. As a kid, I was a big fan of going to the state rodeo (now I do not even care to go).When I was nine years old, one thing my friends and I liked to do was go to the state rodeo together. We begged our parents to take us to meet and watch those professional bull riders get thrown around as they tried to stay on the bull for eight seconds.

We also went to the state rodeo to hear the best country music performer to come that year, to get the flashing light sticks, and to run around in the dirt. Back then, it was fun, and we didn't mind getting covered in dirt. Now, I would rather stay home.

Being nine years old and sick was not fun. But being nine years old, sick, and potentially missing a fun night with your friends at the rodeo was traumatizing. I had a wake-up call as I lay there on what felt like my deathbed. I needed to get better to go to the rodeo by Friday night. The calendar said Wednesday, so I knew I had time. I did what I could to get well.

The main obstacle I had to overcome was the high fever. I thought to myself, "I feel like I am on fire. What puts out a fire? Cold water!" I gathered strength to get myself off the couch and to the nearest shower. Usually, I like a warm shower, but this time was different. Once I got to my parents' bathroom, I went to their shower and set it on the coldest setting possible. I turned the shower nozzle and ran my hand through the water spraying out of the shower head. 'Yep," I thought, "that is cold."

Now I needed the strength to force myself into what I thought was water coming from Antarctica. My choice was either sweat and not get to go to the rodeo or freeze and maybe get to go. Neither were great options, but I had to decide because the rodeo with my friends was on the line. I was determined to beat this sickness and have fun with my friends.

I stepped into the shower and immediately shivered. Saying I was cold was an understatement. I felt like I had just become Frosty the Snowman's best friend. Being hot from a massive and dangerous fever was not my problem. Turning into a block of ice was the newest threat to my rodeo plans.

Staying in the cold shower did not last long. I stayed in there just enough to avoid freezing to death. I turned off the water, stepped out of the shower, dried off, and took my temperature. The thermometer read 100 degrees. Still not enough to convince my parents that I was ready to leave the house. Therefore, I turned the water back on and stepped back into the cold water.

This time, I stayed there slightly longer than the first shower. Yes, I froze and had a miserable time. But I had to be with my friends. I stayed in just a little longer until I could not take it anymore. I then repeated the same process so I could see what my temperature was. This time, the thermometer dropped again and read 99 degrees.

Perfect! The normal temperature is 98.6 degrees Fahrenheit. Surely my current temperature would convince my parents that I was feeling better. Once dressed, I sprinted into the living room to find one of my parents. Mom was the first person I saw, and I showed the thermometer to her. "Look, Mom," I said excitedly, "my temperature is down! "Even though my temperature was down, my mom was not buying my story. She knew what I was doing in the bathroom and told me I could not base the decision on my temperature after a cold shower.

It was a sad moment, but I knew my mom was right. She was looking out for what was best for me and best for those around me. But there was hope as she told me that I could go to the rodeo on Friday if I continued to get better.

Time went by, and my condition continued to get better. Finally, I regained my strength and energy to complete my missed class assignments. I no longer found myself lying on the couch, unable to keep anything in my stomach. Once that Friday rolled around, I felt back to my usual self. Finally, I had just enough energy and a low enough fever to hear my mom say, "You can go to the rodeo tonight."

I was back to my usual self. I went to school the following week and acted like a typical nine year old. However, it was only a matter of time until my life changed permanently.

I was Back to Normal, but...

It had been six weeks since I healed from a week of sickness. Finally, I felt like my usual self again. Then, I woke up one morning before school and, "Ahhhh!" I noticed lots of hair covered my pillow.

I showed my parents, who were just as confused as I was. No one knew what was happening and why I had lost so much hair. So naturally, we began to ask each other questions and replayed a few moments that could have caused me to lose my hair. We asked, "Did my high fever and sickness cause me to lose hair?" I even wondered if my head rubbed against the pillow too hard. The possibilities of why I had hair covering my pillow were endless.

After a few moments of discussing what happened, my mom, dad, and I agreed that the culprit as to why I had hair covering my pillow was that I had worn a Mississippi State Bulldogs cap I got as a gift for my birthday. Being a Mississippi State fan is essential, and I had to represent my favorite college in Mississippi and my favorite team in the Southeastern Conference (SEC). We thought I had worn the cap so much that the strap on the back rubbed so much against my head and was causing hair to fall out.

Once we settled on this agreement, I sprinted to find that hat. I looked all over the house to find the potential cause of my hair loss. I quickly found it and then proceeded to walk outside to the garage so I could throw the cap away. I wanted nothing to do with that cap and did not want to wear it anymore. I love Mississippi State and want to wear their apparel as much as possible, but if the cap caused my hair to fall out, I would sacrifice my passion for my appearance.

Going to school that morning was nerve-racking. I knew I had a bald spot on the back of my head, and I did not want anyone to discover my condition. The thought of embarrassment was too much to handle. However, I knew I had two friends I could trust.

Once I found my friends, I told them what had happened that morning, then showed them what was happening with my hair on the back of my head. They were comforting but also too loud. Finally, one of my friends covered my head and said, "Nothing to see here!" My internal reaction was, "Geez, thanks for the embarrassment." After that, whenever we would walk the hallways, my friend would continue to cover the back of my head. I wanted to keep my problem a secret, but my caring young friend unwittingly made it obvious.

As the days continued, I noticed more hair falling out. Indeed, it was not my Mississippi State hat causing more hair loss because I'd stopped wearing it. "What is going on?!" I thought.

The amount of hair loss drew attention from my parents, too, and we began researching reasons for hair loss while booking appointments with any specialist in the area we could find. For the next few weeks, it felt like I saw a new doctor daily. Instead of being a normal nine-year-old playing sports outside at a friend's house after school, I was going to see a new doctor. My friends lived normal lives while I felt like mine was out of control. It felt like I was losing who I was.

I had lots of blood drawn to see if doctors could identify any problem inside my body. When I was home, I was not even playing with my wrestling action figures after finishing my homework. Instead, I sat in my baseball chair as my mom rubbed steroid cream over my head. I hated it so much. I hated what was happening to me. I did not want to be in that position. I wanted to be normal and keep my hair. Instead, I was sitting in a chair, shirtless, so the cream on my head that was supposed to stimulate hair growth would not drip onto my shirt and ruin it. I felt embarrassed.

It took time for us to figure out what was happening. We had booked appointments with what felt like every doctor in Jackson, MS. Every visit ended similarly. We always left the doctor's office with the words, "We are not sure, but here is our recommendation." From there, it was off to the store to purchase the cream or medicine the doctor said could stimulate the scalp to enable my hair to grow back.

The more we tried, the more my hair fell out. I was losing something that made me who I was. My mom had always said, "Bishop has the straightest dark brown hair I have ever seen." Even when I still had all my hair, I felt I could never settle on a cool-looking hairstyle. What I didn't know then was that even though I could not figure out what hairstyle looked best, it was still better than being a nine-year-old with hair falling out every day. I was not becoming bald as an older man. I was becoming bald as a third grader.

The more my hair fell out, the more questions I had. The more my hair fell out, the more I felt depressed. Very few, if any, questions were being answered. We eventually ran out of help in Jackson, MS, and had to look elsewhere. Our research of potential hair loss specialists led us to Birmingham, AL. Finally, we found a doctor who could potentially give us the answers to why I was losing my hair at such a young age.

Therefore, we made the three-hour journey from the Jackson, MS, area to Birmingham, AL. Everything seems so blurry now as I reflect on that day. The elephant in the room while riding in the car with my nervous parents was a feeling of uncertainty. Would we find the answers to our many questions? Will my hair ever grow back?

We eventually made it to the doctor's office. I recall the building sitting on top of a high hill in Birmingham. As I waited for the doctor to enter the room, I could see the busy interstate below me. Watching the cars helped pass the time. I did everything I could to calm my anxiety. It had been such a long road of receiving little to no answers. It felt like we were losing hope. The never-ending nights of sitting in a chair in the living room with cream covering my head had taken a toll on my emotions. Spending my afternoons in doctors' offices instead of friends' houses felt like missing out on childhood memories.

Then, the doctor walked into the room. The anticipation was building as we hoped she had the answer to what was going on. My parents and I turned our attention to what she had to say. Finally, we were ready to receive the news and discuss my condition with her.

As she sat down, my parents and I explained what brought us here. I was missing school to explain to someone I did not know who lived in a different state that I am a nine-year-old third grader who is losing lots of hair daily. Living this way was not normal, and I wanted to know what was going on with my hair. I wanted to find a way for my hair to grow back.

Conversations continued as we explained that this was not normal. We never had any family sickness or condition passed down from older generations. Anytime I went to the doctor, my results from annual check-up procedures came back normal. I was not allergic to anything and did not struggle with any mental conditions. I was as normal and healthy as a nine-year-old could be.

That was until I experienced the dreaded sickness after my ninth birthday. While it was an agonizing week, I recovered and was back to normal. However, the doctor became intrigued when we explained the experience and told her that my fever had gotten up to 104 degrees. She began to ask questions as to what I experienced while being sick. I gave her my best answers and told her it was awful, but I that I was well again.

After our conversation about my terrible sickness, we finally heard the news we had waited months to hear. No doctor had given us a firm diagnosis of why I was losing hair until now. Finally, the doctor explained that I had alopecia. According to the National Institute of Health, alopecia is "a disease that happens when the immune system attacks hair follicles and causes hair loss."[4] She had reviewed previous test results I received in Jackson, MS, and confirmed my diagnosis.

Naturally, we had many questions, with the first being, "How could I have gotten alopecia?" The doctor said something to the extent of, "Alopecia does not have a cause or cure. If I had to guess, I think the sickness with the high fever after your ninth birthday could have caused your hair loss, as this can happen a month to six weeks after a major sickness." I will never know the exact cause of my alopecia, but one of my first guesses was my 104-degree fever.

Our second question was, "What could we do to fix this problem?" Again, the doctor looked at us with little to no answer and said, "If I knew the cure for alopecia, I would not be here. I would be on a private island in Hawaii."

---

[4] U.S. Department of Health and Human Services. (2024, September 6). *Alopecia areata*. National Institute of Arthritis and Musculoskeletal and Skin Diseases. https://www.niams. nih.gov/health-topics/alopecia-areata

A Wake-Up Call

At the beginning of this chapter, I talked about wake-up calls. Now, I truly recognize one of the most significant wake-up calls in my life. That one visit to that doctor in Birmingham, AL, changed my life forever. I walked out of the doors of that building and got back in the car with my parents. I would be bald for the rest of my life. It was awful and heartbreaking. How would I live my life this way?

I know losing my hair is not the worst thing to ever happen. I know many more who have it worse than me. However, at that moment, it felt like my world had ended. I dreaded what was coming next. Would people accept me? Would I ever look good enough to score a date? Would I be confident looking this way for the rest of my life?

Life is tough and full of moments that challenge us. It takes a wake-up call for us to determine our next action plan. What I believe is one of the biggest wake-up calls in the Bible is one you have probably read multiple times but may not have grasped as a wake-up call.

Matthew 27 explains in detail the crucifixion of Jesus. Towards the end of the chapter, Jesus finally gave His Spirit up to God and passed away. As the earth began to shake and the skies turned dark, Jesus took His last breath. The wake-up call in Matthew 27 happens in verse 54 when the Roman centurion standing near Jesus's cross said, "Surely He was the Son of God."

To understand why this was a wake-up call moment, arguably one of the biggest in the Bible, you must recognize what the centurion and others had done. They had just killed Jesus, who claimed to be God's Son. Jesus had performed miracles and brought the dead back to life. He had spoken of a new kingdom that was coming. Now, it seemed, over.

Then, the earth revolted. As the Roman centurion watched what was happening around him, he realized what he had just done. He probably thought what he and his companions had done was unforgivable. The Son of God hung lifeless on the cross. It took that image of Jesus for this Roman centurion to wake up and admit that he had just helped to kill God's Son.

I love the way Got Questions Ministries explains this experience. They say, "The eyewitnesses recognized that this was no ordinary death and no ordinary man. The things Jesus said were true, and He was who He claimed to be. It is remarkable that the centurion recognized Jesus's true identity and that he did so when Jesus died. Some refused to recognize Jesus as the Son of God even after He rose from the dead. This centurion and those who were working with him recognized because of what Jesus said and what they saw that 'Truly this was the Son of God.'"[5]

What is your wake-up call moment? What has changed you? My hair loss and the new diagnosis changed me and my appearance forever. As I continue to tell my story, you will see that I had major hurdles to overcome. I struggled for the next few years with my confidence and ability to accept my new life. But, looking back now, it was a wake-up call to something better.

A wake-up call moment is meant to stimulate a change in your life. It is intended to make you change what you are doing. It can be as simple as a wake-up call in the early morning. Or it can be as severe as your spouse telling you, "It is me or your problems." Whatever your wake-up call moment is, you must decide your next action.

As my story continues, you will see that my reliance on God was the main thing that gave me hope to press forward and accept who I am. My new condition was a wake-up for me to surrender myself to rely on God to get me through the hard times. Without God, I would have no joy and no hope in such a dark place and time.

Relying on God is not always easy....

---

[5] GotQuestions.org. (2022, August 17). *Truly this was the Son of God.* https://www.gotquestions.org/truly-this-was-the-Son-of-God.html

Chapter 3
A New Look

Mirror, mirror on the wall…does my value change based on the opinions of all? Do their views make my worth rise or fall? I learned the long, hard, bald-in-third-grade way that if we rely on what others see and think of us, then we will only see ourselves through their eyes. We will not see ourselves as we truly are. We will only live in the affirmation of others. That is a dangerous place to live.

People may see you as the hometown hero on the football team or as someone who has the potential to make a difference in this world. Sometimes those who have gone before us may encourage us by saying, "I see a bright future for you. God has big plans for you. You are going to do great things!"

Other times, people may not see our potential. For example, a coach may tell us we do not have what it takes to reach the next level. Their words crush our dreams. Others may see us amounting to nothing because of our past mistakes. People may see us as an enemy, or we may see others through hateful eyes.

Even if we do not know someone, we can quickly judge them. You can look at people and immediately think, "They smell," or "They must be poor." How many times have you looked at homeless people on the side of the road and immediately thought, "They are so lazy. They put themselves in this position. Go get a job."?

If you drive into a neighborhood and notice some mansion-sized houses, your first thought is most likely, "Whoever lives there must be rich." You might see the family playing a game outside their home and gaze at what they are wearing. You notice they have the finest designer clothes, shoes, and jewelry. Their hair is perfectly combed, and their teeth are the perfect shade of white. What is your first thought? "Wow! They are rich."

Again, everyone has a perspective on others. We naturally compare ourselves to others. We try to put ourselves above people to the best of our abilities because our flesh wants to be perceived as the greatest. It frustrates most of us to know that someone is above us.

I love the story of how Thomas Edison's mom did not let one note define her son's future. Of course, there is debate about whether this story is true. But this story still teaches us the importance of not letting others define who we are.

> One day Thomas Edison came home and gave a paper to his mother. He told her, "My teacher gave this paper to me and told me to only give it to my mother."
>
> His mother's eyes were tearful as she read the letter out loud to her child: "Your son is a genius. This school is too small for him and doesn't have enough good teachers for training him. Please teach him yourself."
>
> Many years later, after Edison's mother had died, he was looking through old family things. Now one of the greatest inventors of the century, he suddenly saw a folded piece of paper in the corner of a desk drawer. He took it and opened it up. On the paper was written: "Your son is addled [mentally ill]. We won't let him come to school anymore."
>
> Edison cried for hours and then he wrote in his diary: "Thomas Alva Edison was an addled child that, by a hero mother, became the genius of the century."[6]

In my life, I struggled with how others perceived and defined me. After I lost my hair, I was subject to stares, confusion, and bullying – and it wrecked me. Anytime I was out in public, I wanted to wear a hat. I wanted to hide my baldness because I was afraid to show my condition. However,

---

[6] Tomhasker. (2023, February 5). *How Thomas Edison's mother was the making of him.* Lighthouse Community. https://www.lighthousecommunity.global/post/how-thomas-edison-s-mother-was-the-making-of-him

I knew I had to eventually overcome this fear. Therefore, I pushed myself in small increments at a time. I challenged myself to leave my hat in the car when I would go Walmart shopping with my mom. I would walk tensely into Walmart, knowing someone would stare at me, and they did. Other children my age, who had full heads of hair and were shopping with their moms as well, could not take their eyes off me. Their deadlock stares made me more self-conscious.

My head would drop in embarrassment. Then I would turn to my mom to look for affirmation that I should not be embarrassed of myself. As I sought her approval and love, I would catch her with an intense stare back at the children who could not take their eyes off me. Seeing my mom with her protective stare made things worse. I would say, "Mom, quit staring at those children." She would reply, "Well, they need to stop staring at you."

It was not easy for my Mom to see me hurting. It was not easy for me to accept my new identity as the hairless 9-year-old boy. It was obvious that everyone noticed my new 'look.' Not only did I struggle with how others perceived me, but I also struggled with how I viewed myself. We may not all look or act alike, but we can relate to the struggle of worrying too much about how others see us and how it affects how we define ourselves. Remember, the worst critic in your life is yourself. I struggled with accepting who I had become.

An Emotional Ride

My new look took some getting used to because I was so young. I didn't know how to cope with what I felt or how to put words to it all. I knew I was not supposed to look like this. Everyone around me had hair. I was the standout in the crowd, which was hard to accept. It was hard to be noticed, and, decades later, it is still hard. I subconsciously realized (and still think) that I am the first person my family and friends look for when pinpointing others in a crowd. My new shiny head made me a visual target and my new identity played on my emotions.

I wanted to hide who I was because I was uncomfortable showing my true self to the public. I tried my best to hide from my friends because I was unsure how they would perceive me. I did not want to meet anyone new unless I had a hat on and was certain I did not have to take it off.

Meeting someone new was especially scary. One day, I met the son of one of our family friends. I knew meeting him was unavoidable. Something that would've excited me previously now made me nervous and shy and embarrassed. Surely, he would notice that I looked different from everyone else. I tried to face my fears as best as I could. As I met this kid, my first words to him were, "Hi, my name is Bishop. I have alopecia." My introduction probably brought more attention to my hair loss condition than it would have if I had not mentioned having alopecia, but I felt a need to get out in front of any questions or comments that he might've had about my appearance.

Everything was new to me. How I interacted with people and dressed in the morning was new. I did not have to wake up and brush my hair or spend a few extra minutes in the shower, shampooing my hair. I no longer had the amusement of laughing at myself in the mirror because of how messy my hair was after sleeping all night. I stopped going to a barber because there was no need to go anymore. It was almost like I was a new person. I had to face a new reality and accept my new appearance. But it was hard and weighed on my emotions.

Going out in public was challenging and something I dreaded after my diagnosis. My young self was not confident enough in who I was. I expected people to look at me funny and curiously. People expect a bald person to be older. It seemed like no one expected to see a bald nine-year-old. I learned that other third graders do not expect to see someone their age without hair. To them, it was like I was from another planet.

Their stares and pointed fingers destroyed my confidence. After all, I was the same friend they'd known all their lives, but now they were looking at me as if I was a stranger. I felt like a stranger. I wanted to cry and hide whenever I saw someone my age staring at me.

I tried to hide my look as much as I could. However, I would wear a hat almost everywhere I went. Finally, my parents and I talked with the elementary school administrator about allowing me to wear a hat in the classroom. While wearing hats was not allowed, the administration made an exception for me because they knew I was struggling and was not confident in my new look.

I did not just wear a hat to school. I also wore a hat to church. When my family and I visited a new church, I wore a hat because I feared others' perceptions of me. Of all places, I should be accepted at church for who I am, but I was afraid to show people at church my new look because I was fearful of judgment and stares. Losing my hair played on my emotions so much that I was scared to express my true self at the one place where I should have done so.

I had the option of being noticeable because of not having hair or being recognized for being the only person wearing a hat in church one Sunday morning. I chose to wear a hat because I felt more secure in hiding than expressing who I was, even in church. Sure, I was noticeable, but I was also comfortable hiding under the brim of a hat.

While I felt secure in hiding my new look, I did have an awkward moment the first time we visited this church near Jackson, MS. Before the main church service, my parents dropped me off in a classroom with kids my age. Not only was I dealing with being noticeable for wearing a hat in church, but now I had to meet new people my age. Lacking in self-confidence, meeting new people was an added stress in my life.

Thankfully, that morning, a peace came over me, which helped me through the class. But the awkward moment came when one of the Sunday school teachers said, "We need to pray before we leave." The other teacher looked at me and said, "We take hats off when we pray." Of course, there was no chance I would take my hat off. I shyly went over to where she was sitting and whispered in her ear, "I have a problem and cannot take my hat off." She understood and let me keep my hat on during the prayer. I am thankful for this teacher's empathy and understanding because this whole experience was uncomfortable and could've been more so.

It was not just the stares and potential judgment that crushed me and destroyed my confidence. Words also hurt. The phrase, "Sticks and stones may break my bones, but words will never hurt me," did not ring true for me. Unfortunately, the judgmental words hurt worse than a broken bone.

One day, in fifth grade, I was on the playground with my friends. At this time in my journey of accepting that I had alopecia, I was no longer wearing a hat to school or church (more on this story in chapter four). Even though I eventually became comfortable with my new look, I was not pleased with having people stare at me or make rude and hurtful comments about me. On this day in fifth grade, I experienced an interaction that was a turning point in my journey.

I recall vividly that it was a nice, sunny day. Little to no clouds were in the sky, and my friends and I were enjoying a beautiful day on the playground. We sat around the playground, having a friendly and pleasant conversation about random things fifth graders talk about. As we were talking, I felt a little pebble hit me. Then two more struck my body after that. I looked around to notice a kid sitting away from us. He was the one throwing those pebbles at me.

Once I became aware of his actions, I asked him, "Hey, why are you throwing rocks at me?" His sudden response stunned me. He said, "Because you are bald." Four words are all it took to ruin my day. I will never forget those four words. At this time, I was becoming more confident in who I was and how I looked. However, those four words broke me.

I went home that day and could not stop crying. I sat on my parents' bed and expressed my feelings and emotions to my mom. She tried to comfort me as best as possible, but I was too upset. Words have the power to build up or destroy a person. At that moment, those four words killed me. I was an emotional wreck for much of the afternoon. I felt anger towards God. How could He allow me to lose all my hair? How was I supposed to handle the bullying from others? I was distraught.

After I calmed down, I had a conversation with my mom without crying my eyes out or letting anger control my thoughts, words, and actions. Instead, I began to express my feelings to my mom. We talked about how I could handle the situation if it happened again in the future.

God bless my late grandmother, who died in January 2023. She was a wonderful grandmother and loved each of her grandkids. One thing my grandmother was good at was helping me and her other grandkids when we were in trouble or struggling. She had a genuine heart and loved others. She did not play around when it came to ensuring that we were in good spirits. For example, when I lost my hair, she made a list of potential comebacks for me to use against people who made fun of me for being bald.

My mom and I looked at the list that her mom, my grandmother, gave me. We read through each comeback carefully. Some of these comebacks were crazy. After a thorough look at each one, I found the one reply I knew would help me if this kid started bullying me again.

The next day, I was outside at the playground, having fun with my friends. As I stood watching others running around and sliding down the slides, I heard two words directed at me. The same kid that threw rocks at me the previous day approached me again. He proceeded to say, "Hey, Baldy!" Yes, those words hurt, but this time I had a comeback.

I looked at him and asked, "Would you like to know why I am bald?" I gave him no time for a response so I could know he heard what I had to say next. I continued, "I have cancer. I am going to die in three months." Immediately, this kid was remorseful. Tears began to dwell in his eyes as he apologized multiple times. "I am sorry. I am sorry," he said to me.

He was not the only one that was immediately remorseful, as I felt horrible for lying. I looked at him and said, "I am sorry I had to lie to you, but do not make fun of me." From that point on, he never made fun of me again.

Only God Defines You

Let me address the elephant in the room and say it was not right for me to lie to that kid or be vindictive toward him. While I felt proud for a few moments after watching him cry and apologize, I knew I did not handle the situation in a way that honored God.

I intended to make him feel bad to get revenge. He hurt me, and I wanted to hurt him. I wanted him to feel the pain his words caused me. Yet, I felt nothing but regret when I tried to hurt him. I apologized to him for lying.

Words hurt, and people hurt us. Hurt people hurt people, and we can all classify ourselves as hurting at some point. We all have problems to deal with, and we try to overcome them. We live in a broken world since Adam and Eve failed to obey God's simple command. Therefore, we naturally seek to go against God's order and design for man. When God says, "Love others," we say, "Let's hate others." When God says, "Seek to forgive and reconcile," we say, "Seek revenge and hurt the other person." These are not easy commands because our natural selves do not have the strength to follow what God says on our own. With guidance from the power of the Holy Spirit, we become a reflection of God's loving character. With Jesus in our lives, we can take comfort in being defined as children of God and not by the hateful words of others. We believe Jesus knows us beyond our sins, beyond our appearances, and beyond our feelings.

While my response to the kid who threw rocks at me and addressed me as "baldy" was not Christ-honoring, I am not defined by that sin. The good news for Christians is that we are not defined by what others say about us, nor are we defined by the sins we commit. Does this mean we should continue to sin? No. It does mean that Jesus sees something of value worth dying for; therefore, if we choose to follow Him, Jesus will forgive us, and we will spend eternity with Him.

People may call you names and everyone will form opinions of you. While working at a church, a staff member told me, "It does not take long for people to write your story." We naturally have opinions and will eventually express those opinions to others.

First impressions can shape how others view and think of you. At first glance, people may see you in a positive manner. They may say things like, "She is pretty," or "He must work out." Unfortunately, people may also negatively view you with thoughts such as, "She is so disgusting," or "He is so trashy." Words hurt, and it can be hard to contain your anger when someone lies about you or downgrades you.

I have learned to find peace in how God defines me instead of how others define me. You may have a genuine, caring, and respectful attitude and still, not everyone will see you as such. Isn't it funny how we can be told by nine out of ten people that we are so kind and have great attitudes, but then that tenth person says something different? Whose opinion do we worry about? That tenth person.

One person in the Bible who faced ridicule and lies from others is David. David was the man that slayed a giant. He was the man who committed adultery, but God saw him as a "Man after my own heart" (1 Samuel 13:14, NIV). David was the king. He also is in the lineage of Jesus, God's Son.

Yet, people lied about David and people turned against him. In multiple Psalms that he wrote, David expressed his pain to God when his son betrayed him. David's son, Absalom, lied about him and caused trouble for

David. Absalom caused David so much trouble and fear that he had to flee for his life.

David was anointed king of Israel but had to flee from his town because people had the wrong impression of him. If anyone was to be angry enough to plot revenge against those who inflicted pain on him, it should have been David. Maybe David had a grandmother with a list of comebacks for him to use against others.

A few days before working on this chapter, I read Psalm 62 for my quiet time. Sitting in solitude in my room, I read David's words, meditated on them, and tried to listen as God spoke through His powerful Word. The first eight verses read:

1 Truly my soul finds rest in God;
my salvation comes from him.
2 Truly he is my rock and my salvation;
he is my fortress; I will never be shaken.
3 How long will you assault me?
Would all of you throw me down—
this leaning wall, this tottering fence?
4 Surely, they intend to topple me
from my lofty place;
they take delight in lies.
With their mouths they bless,
but in their hearts they curse.
5 Yes, my soul, find rest in God;
my hope comes from him.
6 Truly he is my rock and my salvation;
he is my fortress, I will not be shaken.
7 My salvation and my honor depend on God
he is my mighty rock, my refuge.
8 Trust in him at all times, you people;
pour out your hearts to him,
for God is our refuge. (NIV)

As you can tell by reading David's words, he was hurt. People were out to get David and destroy him. But where did David find rest? He found rest in God. David had the choice of where his soul found peace. He could have listened to what others said about him, but he realized his soul could only find rest in Christ. When others tried to destroy David, he turned to God and pleaded to Him.

David's way of handling how others defined him is respectable and encouraging. It is one we should model. Others do not define you because you can find rest in God and know that you are a child of God. Your soul may be weary now because of what others say about you. True peace occurs when we release those hurtful words to God. People's words and actions towards you may bless or curse you. When you view yourself through the eyes of God, no matter what they say, your weary soul finds rest.

Come to Jesus with your hurts and burdens. Do not let others define you. Let your soul find the rest it needs and delight in your eternal Father's loving and uplifting words. Others may define you as worthless. But Jesus sees tremendous worth in you. He sees so much value in you that the price He paid for you was His life.

I do not know about you, but if someone paid for me with His life, I want to hear what He says about me.

Chapter 4
Angry at God

Famous theologian and writer Charles Spurgeon said, "Do not say, 'I cannot help having a bad temper.' Friend, you must help it. Pray to God to help you overcome it at once, for either you must kill it, or it will kill you. You cannot carry a bad temper into heaven." American missionary, author, and radio personality John C. Broger said, "Anger and bitterness are two noticeable signs of being focused on self and not trusting God's sovereignty in your life. When you believe that God causes all things to work together for good for those who belong to Him and love Him, you can respond to trials with joy instead of anger or bitterness."[7]

Have you ever been angry at God? A hard pill to swallow is knowing that God does not work on our timetable nor does He operate according to what we want. Isaiah warns us of this, yet we still think God should do as we want. Isaiah 55:8-9 (NIV) says, "For my thoughts are not your thoughts, neither are your ways my ways," declares the Lord. As the heavens are higher than the earth, so are my ways higher than your ways and my thoughts than your thoughts." Paul says in Romans 8:28 (NIV), "And we know that in all things God works for the good of those who love Him, who have been called according to his purpose."

When I read those two verses, I conclude that God knows more than I do, and He is working things out in my life. Therefore, it will be good, and I should trust what He has planned even if I cannot see it. After reading these and thinking those thoughts, I still then thought about how great it

---

[7] Wellman, P. J. (2015, December 8). *42 quotes about anger.* ChristianQuotes.info. https://www.christianquotes.info/quotes-by-topic/quotes-about-anger/

would be if everything worked out the way my planned scenarios played out in my head.

Did you catch that? Did you see what I did there? I first trusted in God, but in the next moment I let my selfishness and flesh get in the way of God's plan. In my mind, I had two options. Option one, I could trust God and abide by His plans. Or option two, I could put myself above God and seek my desires, my way.

Every human has the same options when it comes to being angry at God. Not having God physically present can frustrate us. In the same frustration, we forget that God is working in us and that the Holy Spirit gives us the power to obey God in His Word. That frustration turns to bitterness and leads us further away from seeing the clear picture of God's actions in our lives. The further away you get, the harder it is to see clearly and know how to return.

Anger with God sometimes feels justifiable but should return us to humility. When we see beyond our anger, we are humbled by the fact that it is not God who has done wrong. It is we who have put ourselves above an all-knowing God. We lose every time we try to place ourselves above an all-mighty God.

I will never forget the beginning stages of accepting my hair loss. It came with being humbled by my anger. When I was younger, I was furious with God for taking away my hair. The stares, the bullying, and the insecurity in my identity had me at the end of my rope. It was a tough transition, but I am proud to stand here today and say I overcame it.

It was not easy to overcome, though. I had to find the strength to tell myself that my worth is not found in my appearance. Perhaps you are reading this and have a glaring issue with your appearance. Maybe you are jealous of how others look, dress, or talk. Perhaps you are angry with God because you are in a financial crisis and see no way out. Crying out to God seems repetitive and has worn you down. You are emotionally spent.

I have found that it is comforting to acknowledge that you are not alone. Every Christian, at some point, has expressed built-up anger and frustration against God. If God is so knowing, why does it feel like He does not know we are hurting? Why does it feel like we have not moved, but He has? If we could see the future, then we would be happy. If we knew what would happen after the struggle, we would have less stress in the fight. If we knew how pain would be healed, we would have less anger at God for not healing us sooner. Is the knowledge worth losing God? Why would we need God if we knew everything?

Knowing what I know about my life and hair loss now, I would be a fool to give it all up – recognition of the outcome of a situation that challenges faith strengthens our dependence on God. Looking back, we realize we were the ones who got angry when we should have abided in God. The night I got mad at God for taking my hair away was when I realized God had a bigger plan.

My Hatred for God

I was at my breaking point when I got angry with God. It had been a long journey since I heard the pediatric dermatologist in Birmingham, AL, tell me I had alopecia. Even worse, it seemed like an eternity since I'd had a full head of hair. I was tired of the special creams I rubbed on my head to supposedly stimulate hair growth. I was fed up with people staring at me and laughing at me. My self-confidence diminished as I looked around at what I considered a sea of normal people who had hair.

Finally, one night, I let months of frustration come out. In my furious anger, I told God how I felt. I stood in one of the living rooms of my house and yelled loudly, "I hate you, God!" That's not all. I then had a table-turning moment when I grabbed the nearest object, which happened to be a standing television tray, and launched it across the living room. The end of my rope snapped, and I could not take it anymore. Everything I tried to overcome was destroyed by the hair specialist saying, "There is no known cause or cure for alopecia."

The road came to a dead end. Instead of light at the end of the tunnel, it felt like continual darkness. Eventually, I had no choice but to accept who I was. I tried to do everything possible not to accept this reality. Finally, when I realized there was nothing left to try, I let go of months of anger at God.

After yelling, "I hate you, God," I truly believed it. I wanted nothing to do with prayers and praises. He took my hair, my normalcy, my identity from me, and I felt there was no explanation. Why did I have to suffer embarrassment? It was degrading to watch people stare at me because I looked different from them. It was embarrassing to wear a hat in places like church when no one else was wearing one. Church members wore their Sunday best while I couldn't avoid showing people my Sunday worst.

The night I yelled, "I hate you, God," was liberating. I let out months of built-up disappointment in four simple words. Were they the most thoughtful words or the most God-honoring words? No, they were not. Psalm 19:14 (NIV) says, "May these words of my mouth and this meditation of my heart be pleasing in your sight, Lord, my Rock and my Redeemer." Yet, in one moment of unleashing anger, I failed to let my words be pleasing to God. Yes, I believe God is my Rock and Redeemer, but I allowed my bitterness and my finite mind overcome my faith that God controls my life and this world.

A few minutes passed after I threw that television tray across our living room. Luckily, I did not throw it hard and far enough to break the sliding glass door to our back porch patio. Still, I just could not take it anymore. The bitterness continued to build until the anger came out. Once it was out, I felt free – until shame and regret grew.

I realized the error of my ways and knew I did not handle my situation well. Psalm 55:22 (NIV) talks about remaining calm during life's storms when it says, "Cast your cares on the Lord, and He will sustain you; He will never let the righteous be shaken." I neglected to cast my cares on the Lord. Instead, I buried them inside until I could not handle them anymore. I was learning that buried things are not dead things – they come back up and out.

Still, I felt free as I finally expressed how I was really feeling. My anger soon led to regret as I said four words I hope never to utter again. I finally calmed down and took a deep breath. I picked up the television tray and returned it to where it belonged. Later that night, I went with my mom to run a few errands. On the way home, I remembered praising God as we listened to the local Christian radio station.

I find it ironic that in one day I went from hating God to praising Him. It shows the beauty in failure. When handled correctly, we can grow in strength and perseverance as we face trials. My favorite non-Christian band, Alter Bridge, recognizes this truth in their song, "My Champion."

The lyrics say, "But failures made are lessons learned." I failed when I spoke those harsh words to God. I needed to learn that my fight against alopecia was the beginning of shaping me into who I am today.

The Unanswered Questions

Sometimes it seems that God never answers our questions. Instead, we focus on our problems as if God does not care. It may seem that everyone around you is experiencing blessings while you are constantly waiting on God to answer your prayers. Living in a world where we showcase our best while hiding our worst creates a false narrative. We have manipulated our minds to believe that God is bestowing blessings on not only the Christians we know but also the people who seem to get away with all sorts of evil.

Questioning God is not a new concept, and we aren't the only ones who have. Great leaders and followers of Jesus in the Bible struggled to trust God when it seemed they were not receiving answers to their questions. Job is perhaps the most remarkable example of this in the Bible. The opening chapters of Job give the readers an inside look at a conversation between God and Satan. Who was not part of that conversation and was never told about it? Job.

One thing that annoys me is when people volunteer me for a project or say I can do something without consulting me first. No one consulted Job or asked his opinion about being put through so many trials, including his own children dying. God did not need Job's approval before agreeing with Satan that he could test Job's faith. God knew Job better than Satan did, and God knew Job better than Job knew himself.

God knows what you can and cannot handle. All is done in His perfect timing, and it's for the best, even when we don't see that. Everything God does goes according to the plans He laid out. Psalm 75:2 (NIV) says, "You say, 'I choose the appointed time; it is I who judge with equity.'" God's plans for Job did not depend on Job's answers, and God's plans for your life do not depend on your approval. Paul writes in Romans 9 about the potter's rights to the clay. The potter knows how to form and shape the clay. In the same way, God knows what He is doing when He is forming and shaping you.

It is incredibly tough to go through hard times and face challenges you thought you would never deal with. My dad always tells me, "Life will hit you in the mouth." He talks to me about how our response to hardship forms our character. Life is full of inevitable adversities. This book is my story of facing an adversity in my life that is evident and seems to have no cure. In addition, I hope the contents of this book will help to open your eyes and heart to God's creation staring back at you in the mirror. That person in the reflection of the mirror is valuable in God's eyes. No adversity can take away what God is forming.

Each of us will face challenges in life. We will all have moments where we cry out what Job cried in Job 3:3 (NIV), "May the day of my birth perish, and the night that said, 'A boy is conceived.'" For most of the book of Job, we read about his challenges and how he and others responded. It is not until the end of the book that we read God's response to Job. Remember, God approved of the testing and trials Job faced. He could have told Job, "I approved of this because I knew you would still have faith in me."

Job had questions for God, as many of us do. We want to know why there is suffering in the world and why God would permit such atrocities to happen in life. Sometimes our prayers to God tend to be focused on our issues as we ask God for an explanation. Just like in Job's situation, God knows the answers as to why you are suffering. Look again in the mirror and realize that you may not have the solutions to the challenges of your life. But the One whose standard is higher than anyone else's knows what you are going through. You may not have answers and may never have insight into what God was doing this whole time. However, you can look in the mirror confidently, knowing that the One who created you believes in you.

Life, indeed, is problematic because sin has corrupted it. We will continue to face hardships and challenges as we journey through the mysteries of life. Unanswered questions are undesirable. I can only speculate as to why I lost my hair. One thing I take comfort in is when I look in the mirror now versus when I did years ago as a child. I now know I would not trade my situation for anything. My dad one day asked me if I wanted to take shots in my head to stimulate hair growth. My response was a stern "No." I will always struggle with feeling different than others. But I also know that the person staring back at me in the mirror is a creation of God.

So, what is unanswered in your life? What struggles are you facing that you want answers to? I can only imagine what others are going through and how angry they must be at God. No one on earth will ever know what you are feeling. Your feelings are between you and God. Job's friends and wife tried to comfort him, but they offered terrible advice. They could never relate to him because they weren't Job. Only Job could relate to himself just like only you can relate to you.

What Job did was something we should do. He expressed his anguish to God. Job came to the end of the rope and cried out to God. I will never forget when I realized that the person staring back at me in the mirror was who I would be for the rest of my life. There will come a time in your pain and trials when God will seem so far off in the distance, and you will cry out to Him to come back. Yet, the distance is not because God moved but because you did. Trials expand our distance from God only when we focus on our suffering rather than our faith. Even in suffering, that distance can shorten, and you can return to God.

After God questioned Job for questioning Him, Job did not get angry. Even though Job had no answers to his sufferings, he realized that God was right and repented (Job 42:1-6). In his Bible commentary, John MacArthur says, "Job's confession and repentance finally took place. He still did not know why he suffered so profoundly, but he quit complaining, questioning, and challenging God's wisdom and justice. He was reduced to such utter humility, crushed beneath the weight of God's greatness, that all he could do was repent for his insolence. Without answers to all of his questions, Job bowed in humble submission before his Creator and admitted that God was sovereign."[8]

May we take a lesson from Job today and repent of questioning God in anger. May we trust that the Potter, God, knows what He is doing when He forms the clay, us. Unanswered questions are inevitable, but the person staring back at you when you look in the mirror can respond in faithful obedience to God's plans rather than anger and distrust.

---

[8] MacArthur, John. "Job," In *The MacArthur Bible Commentary. edited by John MacArthur,* 593. Nashville, TN.: Thomas Nelson, 2005.

Chapter 5
Staring at Reality

Sometimes we just need a good look at ourselves in the mirror to face reality. The title for this book comes from that one night when I knew I had to accept my life for what it was. Nothing was working to get my appearance back to what it was before my alopecia diagnosis. I longed for the days when I had hair. I wanted to look normal. Being bald in the third grade was not something I chose to be. I did not want to live or look this way. Yet, nothing was working to change it.

Part of me felt I wasted a lot of time by going to the doctors. I felt the only thing I did achieve through doctor's visits and temporary remedies was wasted time. My glass was half empty, and I began to lose hope. It took a literal table-flipping moment of rage to express my distaste for what God allowed to happen to me. As discussed in the previous chapter, I felt nothing but hatred for God at that moment.

On that same night, I had an epiphany. I escaped to my parents' bathroom. I did not have an agenda in mind. I just needed to get away. Thankfully, my parents' bedroom and bathroom were in the back of our house. Therefore, as I retreated, I found some alone time. After yelling at God, throwing tables, and proclaiming my hatred for God, I knew walking away from the room where my incident took place would help relieve my anxieties.

The doors to my parents' bathroom extended outwards when opened, and you immediately see two bathroom counters with mirrors. After a night of being upset with God and then praising Him through song, I figured the last thing I wanted to see was myself. I was confused, having gone from hatred in the den to then praising God in the car. I did not understand what was happening in my mind. However, I opened the two doors, and there, in the mirror, was my reflection staring straight at me.

I did not say anything. It was just my reflection and me. Looking in the mirror, it felt like I was looking into my soul. I was searching for who I was. I understood my condition in that moment. It had been months since I was diagnosed with an autoimmune disease that has no known cause or cure. Since then, I had done everything I could to hide who I really was.

There was no more hiding. As I opened the bathroom doors and looked at myself in the mirrors, it felt as if I genuinely saw myself for the first time. For a second, I forgot what I looked like before losing my hair. I took a deep breath and walked toward the bathroom counter.

From there, I stretched my arms out and gripped the end of the counter with the palms of my hands. I looked up again. Did I wish I saw a different reflection? Yes. Did I wish I could have looked up to see a full head of hair on my head? Yes. Did I see any of this? No.

All I saw was the new me. I was a bald nine-year-old boy. I looked deeply into the eyes of an elementary student who knew it was time to decide. I could not keep running anymore. I could not keep hiding who I was. The hats had to come off, and my confidence had to rise. My family and friends were supporting me through this challenging time. The only person who was not helping me was me.

That night, I had to take care of some personal business. I had to make things right with myself. I could not keep hiding my appearance. I could not continue being affected by the stares from strangers and the comments made by immature classmates. I had to accept reality that I am (to this day) a unique person because of my condition.

With my grip firmly grasping the edge of my parents' bathroom counter, I stared deep into my own eyes. Finally, I had a serious look on my face. There was no more time for hiding and no more time left for crying. The times of getting upset with God were over. The times of failing to see how I could use my unique feature as an opportunity for God's glory were done. Still grasping the counter and staring into my eyes, I whispered words I would never forget.

Staring at my reflection in the mirror, I proclaimed, "This is going to be me." Those words changed everything about me. Those liberating words made me grow up. I chose a mature stance to accept what was unique about me. I believe God allows terrible things to happen in our lives to mold and shape us into who He wants us to be. He wants to see our character and dependence on Him grow every day. By saying, "This is going to be me," I felt I was acknowledging for the first time that God has a plan for my life, and part of that plan would include losing my hair.

Here I am, staring in the mirror at my reflection. I was looking at someone who – to this day – lives with this identity change. No one else entered the room that night. Looking back, I felt that God was working amidst a bad night. He knew I needed to handle some personal business. I am unsure what my parents were doing while I stood alone in their bathroom. They were not around. God knew I needed that moment, just Him and me. I did not need any distractions.

It was just God and me that night in my parents' bathroom. It was me staring quietly at myself, crying out to God on the inside. It took courage and strength to look at myself in the mirror and accept that losing my hair was something God knew would happen before I was born. If He ordained it to happen, then I needed to accept it. God even knew what would happen five minutes after I left the bathroom, but I did not. Not knowing what was next, I had to take my first step of faith and rely on God to give me the boldness to show people who I was. People needed to see who I saw in the mirror.

I was learning that my value wasn't tied to my appearance. I could not hide anymore; I didn't want to. I could not cover up my head and be ashamed of what God was to use for my good and His glory. If God was to use my alopecia diagnosis to help someone else, then I had to comply with Him. I had to accept my situation so I could also help others accept themselves. I had to embrace the uniqueness of who I am to God. I could no longer be embarrassed or ashamed of what God permitted to happen to me.

It took a time of anger and rage to bring about that acceptance. That night, when I looked in the mirror, I had to pause. I had to look at my life for what it was and accept that my hair was not coming back; alopecia was here to stay. As a young elementary student, in a classroom where everyone had hair, this was tough to swallow. I stuck out. I was very noticeable in a room of at least twenty other kids. However, knowing what I know now about my life, I would not change my hair loss for anything.

I did not become confident overnight. It took years to accept my new appearance. It took a big step in faith and reliance on God. It is a shame we live in a world where so many people are uncomfortable with themselves. They are too fat or too skinny. They are too ugly. They do not get enough likes on social media. People change their genders to words I have never heard before. People have lost the idea that God created you and me as precious royalty. Your deficiencies are your uniqueness. Your scars tell your story. God did not make a mistake with you and what makes you unique. It took me a while to accept the reality of my hair loss, but once I did, and once I took that step of faith realizing God's workmanship, I found the beauty in my uniqueness.

Get the Shovel and Move the Mountain

I did not recognize the magnitude of how important the story of faith and the mustard seed was until I saw a mustard seed for the first time. To say it is tiny is an understatement. After hearing that story, I thought, "Surely I can have that amount of faith." One day, some friends and I talked about this story in class. We figured we could move mountains and do anything if it took just a tiny amount of faith. Our next thought was, "If we have faith as tiny as a mustard seed, then we can tell the desks in our classroom to move to the opposite side of the room."

We began to speak at the desks. "Move, desk, to the opposite side of the room! Move desk! Move now!" Did the desks move? No. Did we probably look and sound stupid? Most likely. Was our faith not strong enough? It was more likely that we were trying to do something that was about our own selves and not God. I do not know, but I do know that we appeared very weird.

The story of the mustard seed in Matthew 17 is well known and becomes meaningful when we know the whole story. It becomes relatable when we embrace the lesson God wants us to take from it. This story can also be hard to accept when we compare ourselves to the disciples and realize that we, too, have little faith.

Matthew 17 begins with the transfiguration of Jesus. Peter, James, and John followed Jesus to the top of a mountain where He stopped. John MacArthur writes in his Bible commentary that Jesus underwent a "...dramatic change in appearance so the disciples can behold Him in His glory. These three disciples saw Jesus in a form that the other nine disciples did not experience. They witnessed an impressive sight on the mountain, and none wanted to leave. They also heard the voice of God proclaiming Jesus to be His Son. What they saw was magnificent, but Jesus told them not to say anything to anyone."[9]

Peter, James, and John saw Jesus for who He was. They witnessed Jesus in His glory and heard a voice proclaim and affirm that who they saw was God's Son. After witnessing this transfiguration and having spent numerous times with Jesus performing miracles, it would be hard not to have faith in Him and trust His plans for your life.

However, while Jesus spent time on the mountain with Peter, James, and John, the other nine disciples struggled with their faith. Upon their return from the mountain, a man approached them, begging Jesus to heal his son (Matthew 17:14-15). The father said, "I brought him to your disciples, but they could not heal him." The disciples who saw Jesus perform miracles demonstrated their lack of faith and did not trust what God was doing. Instead of having faith in God's power to drive the demon out of the boy, the disciples seemed to rely on their own power. Our power will never be as strong as God's power.

What are you trying to heal on your own? What are you trying to fix with your strength and power? Here are nine Christian men trying to cast out a demon, but none of them succeeded. They relied on their strength and power and ultimately failed. Perhaps you see failure in your battle to overcome a struggle or accept your uniqueness. Amid your struggle, ask yourself, "Where does my faith come from?" Those nine disciples saw Jesus do amazing things and heard Him say "Follow me," and "Have faith." Yet, they failed to rely on this faith in Jesus when the opportunity arose. How often do we do the same thing?

In His grace and mercy, Jesus used this lack of faith to heal the demon-possessed boy and as a teaching moment for His disciples. The disciples demonstrated a lack of trust and reliance on Jesus, but Jesus did not con-

[9] MacArthur, John. "Matthew," In *The MacArthur Bible Commentary*. edited by John MacArthur, 1,156. Nashville, TN.: Thomas Nelson, 2005.

demn them. Their faith continued to develop, just as mine and your faith continues to grow. In our imperfections, Jesus helps us grow closer to Him. There were a lot of unknowns about Jesus at this time, but He continued to teach those people who followed Him.

Jesus calls us to walk with Him daily. In Luke 9:23 (NIV), Jesus describes His faithful followers as those who "deny themselves, take up their crosses daily and follow me." Your faith journey does not end until Jesus calls you home. He created you with a purpose and made you for a reason. Who you are is not a mistake. You are a miracle in the eyes of Jesus.

One of the first steps to accepting your uniqueness is having faith in Jesus. Jesus helped develop His disciples' faith, so He will help you develop your faith. Jesus was not angry with them because He wanted what was best for them. Instead, Jesus wanted them to have faith in Him. Therefore, Jesus helped His disciples to see that it only takes a little faith in God to move the mountains they feared.

Whatever your mountain is right now, it can be moved. Through your faith in Jesus come your works for Him. Your uniqueness has a purpose. If you are doubting what that purpose is, as I did, it is time to take the shovel and start moving that mountain. There comes a time when you must start digging up your mountain using your faith in Jesus. When I looked at myself in the mirror, I realized that my fear of rejection and ridicule for being bald was the mountain in my way. Once I accepted my uniqueness, I knew I had to take the shovel and start digging up my mountain.

God did not leave me alone to do all the work. I believe He wanted me to demonstrate my faith through works and allow Him to take care of the rest. Just like the disciples, I had to learn a lesson as to why faith in myself always fails and why belief in God succeeds. If I continued to rely on myself to overcome my fear of being made fun of or letting others see me as a bald young kid, then that mountain of fear would still be where it was the night I looked at myself in the mirror. I would have walked away from my parents' bathroom mirror, facing shame and embarrassment. I would not have accepted my uniqueness.

Just as the disciples had to learn a lesson for having little faith, so did I. I had a choice. I could walk away in shame and embarrassment of what God permitted to happen in my life, or I could walk away with a shovel in my hand and begin to work on moving the mountain that was in front of me. Today, there may be a mountain in front of you causing you to be scared to let people see you for your true self, who God created you to be. Let me encourage you. There is freedom in placing that shovel into the side of the mountain, digging up that first piece of dirt. After that first step, God will continue to help you dig up the entire mountain until you experience true freedom on the other side.

Even the Greats Struggle to Accept Their Uniqueness

The Bible is full of people who feel insufficient to do God's work. Abraham claimed he was too old to have a child; Rahab was a prostitute; Gideon did not believe in himself; Paul killed Christians. There are countless examples of people in the Bible who told God they were not good enough, but this did not keep God from using them to fulfill His plan. Each of the people God called had a uniqueness about them that they thought would hinder them from being used by God.

The story of Moses leading the Israelites away from Egyptian captivity is one of the most well-known Bible stories. If you grew up in Sunday School, I have little to no doubt that you heard this story at least one hundred times. The story of Moses leading the Israelites to freedom does not impact our lives if we don't remember where Moses came from.

Moses was a murderer. Exodus 2:12 (NIV) tells us that Moses "killed the Egyptian and hid him in the sand." He took a man's life. Today, when people are accused of murder, they lose their freedom. In some areas of this world, the murderer loses the right to life. Whether the one who committed murder faces the death penalty or jail time, loss of freedom is certain.

Not only was Moses a murderer, but he also struggled to speak which caused Moses to doubt himself. God knew the struggles Moses and his people were facing and spoke to Moses as a burning bush in Exodus 3. "I have seen the misery of my people in Egypt. I have heard them crying out because of their slave drivers, and I am concerned about their suffering. So, I have come down to rescue them from the hand of the Egyptians and to bring them up out of that land into a good and spacious land, a land flowing with milk and honey- the home of the Canaanites, Hittites, Amorites, Perizzites, Hivites and Jebusites. And now the cry of the Israelites has reached me, and I have seen the way the Egyptians are oppressing them. So now, go. I am sending you to Pharaoh to bring my people the Israelites out of Egypt" (Exodus 3:7-10, NIV).

God knows what is going on in your life. When He calls you to a task for His glory, He does not make mistakes. He did not choose you by accident – He knows you are the right person for the job. It takes a step of faith to accept what God calls you to do. You might be afraid to acknowledge your uniqueness, choosing instead to hide behind the mountain that stands in the way of what God has for you. You are not alone; many great people in the Bible struggled to take a shovel to their mountain.

Moses was no different when he asked God, "Who am I that I should go to Pharaoh and bring the Israelites out of Egypt?" (Exodus 3:11, NIV) God's response is encouraging and reminds us of His character. He did not directly answer Moses's question. Instead, God replied in a comforting way, "I will be with you" (Exodus 3:12). Who was Moses that God called him to be the leader of His people? Moses was a murderer who was afraid of others and himself. Yet, God wanted Moses to be free of these fears so he could lead His people to freedom. Moses had to be free of his own mountain in order to lead people out of captivity to God's Promised Land.

Moses was a murderer who doubted his ability to be used by God. He questioned God's plans. Moses stuttered when speaking. He lacked in self. Moses described himself in these ways and appeared to dread who he was. He did not want to be used by God because he did not think he was good enough. It may sound discouraging to say that none of us are good enough to be used by God. We are insufficient compared to a sufficient God. However, God is the author of life and knows our struggles. He sees our uniqueness as an opportunity to make His name known. I am encouraged to know that God thinks I am worthy to be used by Him even when I don't believe I am.

Moses eventually led the Israelites to freedom. Moses started his journey with Christ locked away in the doubts of his mind. He knew full well the sins he'd committed. In turn, he hid from others and became trapped in his doubt. His doubt trapped him in beliefs that were not true. But God used this trapped man, who himself needed freedom, to free His people.

God used a man who took another man's life to be a hero to others.

We still read about Moses today and are encouraged by his faith. Moses would be shocked to know how many people his story touches. God helped Moses stop doubting his abilities, which enabled Moses to realize his unique qualities. God fulfilled His promise to guide Moses every step of the way. Today, God is with you. You may feel inadequate or embarrassed with yourself. Where you see ugly, God sees beauty. When you think you have no opportunities to make a difference, God sees potential in you.

I walked away from seeing a bald young kid in the mirror, knowing that I had the potential to be used by God. It took a firm step of faith for me to walk away from the mirror with confidence. But I knew the alternative would be to continue hiding my appearance and being embarrassed. I am thankful that I accepted my uniqueness at that moment. That was just the first step because I still needed the courage to show others who I really was.

It was easy to step out of my parents' bathroom with the courage to face others because my family saw my look every day. With God's help, I overcame the first challenge – accepting myself. The next step was to gain the courage to reveal myself to others. I had to learn how to become comfortable around others. I had to become comfortable walking into public places knowing that strangers would stare at me.

Honestly, I did not want to feel the stares or hear the potential ridiculing jokes. I knew that accepting my identity would be more meaningful if I revealed to others who I truly am. Once I left my parents' bathroom, I had one more challenge to overcome – I had to maintain the courage to be who God made me to be.

Chapter 6
Be Courageously You

One does not find courage in hiding who you are. The courage to accept yourself is not found in faking who you are. The courage to accept who you are is only found in recognizing whose you are. It takes admitting and confessing your brokenness to a holy and loving God. The Bible says that we become new creations when we have the courage to cry out to Jesus for salvation (2 Corinthians 5:17 NIV). I would rather be a new creation in Christ than to try to become a new creation of my own making.

It takes having Jesus inside your heart to realize who you are. He gives you the courage to embrace your new identity as a child of the Most High God. He also gives you the courage to face your most challenging battles. Accepting who you are or what you look like can sometimes be a difficult task. Looking at yourself in the mirror and being pleased with the reflection can be hard. The world will tell you that you are not good or tough enough. You may believe the lies that you are not worthy enough. Right now, you may want to hide who you are.

Letting others see you when you are embarrassed by your appearance is tough. Speaking from first-hand knowledge, I believe it is more beautiful to let people see your scars, hurts, pain, and suffering than to hide behind a mask and pretend to be something you are not.

I could have easily succumbed to hiding who I was. I could have worn a wig or had up to thirty injections in my head to stimulate hair growth. Neither option would have resulted in my natural hair returning, but it would have at least let me hide that I was bald. However, I refused both options because I knew it would have resulted in something I was not. Once

I saw how my condition could be used for God's glory, I knew I needed to embrace my new appearance so God could use me. When I left my parents' bathroom that night and stopped dwelling on my looks, I knew there was a challenge ahead of me.

The first thing I needed to do was accept my new identity. It was not going to be easy, but I needed courage. If I wanted to be comfortable with who I was, I had to accept how God made me and what happened to my hair. Did I have all the answers? No. But I had God on my side, and, as tough as it was to admit, He was all I needed.

The Courage to Show Others

Things did not change overnight. It took some time to accept that there was nothing else to do but realize I probably would be bald the rest of my life. The dreams of growing long hair to look like some of my favorite rockstars or having a full-grown man beard were crushed. However, the hope that this situation would build courage in my life and strengthen my reliance on God was alive. Finally, I accepted that a broken dream from the world is worth it if it means living in the reality of God's plan.

Still, gaining that knowledge and courage was not easy. I had to take life one day at a time as I revealed my true self to the outside world. From time to time, some hair would grow but eventually would fall out. I wanted to keep what hair I could because I knew it would be a struggle to live without any of it. Time, courage, and God's strength reminded me that I am worth so much more than the stares of strangers in public. The strangers' glares hurt, but thankfully that is not where I find my identity. My identity is in Christ and what He thinks about me.

What are you not giving up, or where do you find your identity if it is not in Christ? It takes courage to be honest and admit that you have fallen short of how God sees you. There is freedom in honesty and vulnerability. There is freedom in expressing your struggles to Christ and realizing that your worth is found in God's Words, not your insufficiencies. For example, you may struggle to accept your appearance and fail to see that God made you beautiful because you reflect His image (Genesis 1:27 NIV). When you look at yourself in the mirror, you can either see failure and disgust or the wonderful creation a loving Creator has made.

I was set free when I could look at myself in the mirror and be honest about my condition. I have alopecia; I am bald; there is nothing I can do about it. When something is out of our control, we can either let it affect us mentally or use it as an opportunity to wait patiently on God's plan. Being diagnosed with alopecia at a young age was a hard struggle. However, this misfortune has enabled me to share my story.

I had to face my struggles with alopecia. I could not hide my appearance any longer. Wearing hats to church and school to cover up my embarrassment and fear of being ridiculed would not get me the freedom I wanted. I knew the time would eventually come for me to take the hat off to become comfortable with myself. I just needed a bit more courage.

Thankfully, I gained that courage to leave the house and go to public places, like school and church, without wearing a hat. As I bravely exposed my new appearance and self, people continued to stare at me. However, my confidence in my appearance grew. I knew there was more to me than how the public viewed me. Yes, the comments and stares hurt, but I learned to brush them off more easily because I had been able to accept that God was going to use my alopecia for His glory. Knowing that God is writing the story of my life gave me hope and assurance of my identity in Him. You begin to realize who you are and accept yourself when you know Christ has accepted you.

Romans 5:8 (NIV) tells us, "But God demonstrates His own love for us in this: While we were still sinners, Christ died for us." He accepts us as we are, sinners. Jesus accepts us when we are ashamed of ourselves. This thought speaks to me beyond alopecia because I am not just a person without hair. Instead, I am a bald person who has sinned against a holy, just, and perfect God. The only way God could see me as one of His children would be for me to accept the gift of salvation from His Son. For those who follow Christ, the reflection in the mirror does not determine your value. Your reflection shows a redeemed sinner saved by grace.

Knowing these truths help me in my continuous journey to be my new self to others. To my surprise, my friends accepted me. They did not care what I looked like. They saw beyond my appearance. They saw my character more than my appearance, which is how Jesus sees you. Your value to Jesus is not found in how you look. Instead, your value in Jesus is found in what He did for you on the cross.

My courage continued to grow as I became more comfortable not wearing a hat while in public. Over time, it became easier to be free to be myself. Thankfully, my friends encouraged me to be myself. These friends were aware of my situation and liked me for who I was, not how I looked. I had a great support system with them.

During my middle school years, I experienced random hair growth, then the hair would gradually fall out. I will never forget a time I had some hair on the back of my head and one thin line of hair in the middle of my head. I always hoped that my hair would fully grow back even if it was just a small amount as I had at this time. At one point between the end of eighth grade and the beginning of ninth grade, my head had several patches of hair growing. I had to decide if I wanted to keep the little amount that seemed to be growing or shave the hair entirely off.

As I look back now, I realize the error of my ways. I have seen the pictures of the little hair I had in middle school, and I looked ridiculous. The little bit of hair combed and gelled to the side was not the look I needed. So, believe me when I tell you that it is taking a lot of courage to write this part of my story. I would rather not remember this time. I credit writing this part of my story to looking back at a horrible high school yearbook photo.

After looking at family pictures from a Disney World trip and feeling the embarrassment of them, I realized I needed to do something different. Obviously, I was not aware of how ridiculous I looked. All I can do now is laugh at my hairstyle choice. Through this experience, I gained the courage to laugh at myself more.

For several years, my hair would come and go. As it grew, I knew it was only a matter of time before it would fall out again. Whenever I had that little bit of hair, I wanted to keep it and enjoy it because I knew it was inevitable that I would someday lose it again.

Mostly, only a tiny amount of hair would grow back. The hair would be so thin and light in color that it would be unnoticeable unless you looked closely at my head. I had to patiently and courageously learn to accept this reality and build strength to not get depressed when my hair would grow, only to fall out again. If it meant having a lousy hairstyle, I was willing to risk it because it was the only hair I had. To make things right, I knew I had to shave the patches off completely.

A short time after our Disney World trip, I gained the confidence and courage to shave off the remaining pieces of my hair. Was I sad? No. I was actually happy that I made the decision: shaving my head helped me fully embrace my condition and build the courage I needed to look at myself in a mirror and become comfortable with who I saw.

The Bible is full of flawed people who never get things right, even when they try. When reading different stories of the Bible, you notice a diverse group of situations, stories of failing and healing, stories of redemption and grace. You also read stories of people discouraged by their conditions until they meet Jesus. Once they met Jesus, their courage grew, and their worries about their conditions lessened. The opinions of others did not matter because Jesus made them feel worthy.

A Man Told Me

The story of the woman at the well in John 4 reminds us that Jesus knows us beyond our sins. Jesus was traveling from Galilee to Judea. He could have taken the long way around instead of going the short route through Samaria, a place where some Jews avoided traveling through because of much dissension.[10] Yet, Jesus was not afraid but tired. In the heat of the day, He decided to rest a while beside the well (John 4:6). After traveling for a long time, one might want to sit down and drink water.

It would be ideal to draw water from a well in the morning to avoid the afternoon heat. However, one woman waited until the middle of the day to come to the well, not joining the other women who came in the morning. Instead, she came alone when the sun was scorching hot. Why? Perhaps she needed water, but she knew the other women considered her a social outcast. She came alone to draw water from the community well when, during biblical times, drawing water and chatting at the well was the social highpoint of a woman's day. However, this woman was ostracized and

[10] *Enduring Word Bible Commentary John Chapter 4*. Enduring Word. (2023, April 27). https://enduringword.com/bible-commentary/john-4/

marked as immoral, an unmarried woman living openly with the sixth in a series of men.[11]

This woman thought she would be alone, but Jesus was there also. Jesus spoke with her and told her that he was the Messiah. Little did this woman know that she was one of the first people Jesus revealed His identity to. Reflect momentarily on the love and grace Jesus had on this woman. She was a disgrace and a nobody to society, but now her story is being told. We do not know who thought she was an outcast. But we do know that Jesus saw potential in her. Jesus saw beyond her sin. She needed the courage to accept what Jesus thought of her.

Jesus revealed everything about this woman's life to her. Jesus spoke to her even when it was against the norms. Traditionally, a rabbi would not speak with a woman in public, even his own wife. It was also *very* unusual for a Jewish person of that time to ask a favor or accept a drink from a Samaritan's cup. Jesus's request genuinely surprised the woman. The disciples were also surprised that Jesus spoke to her (John 4:27).[12]

The woman knew there was something special about Jesus and her encounter with him. So she said, "Sir, I can see that you are a prophet" (John 4:19, NIV). She also said, "I know that Messiah is coming. When he comes, he will explain everything to us" (John 4:25, NIV). The woman knew the Messiah was coming, but she did not realize He was right in front of her. She was about to find out.

Jesus simply said in response to this, "I, the one speaking to you, I am He" (John 4:26, NIV). Here we have a woman who knew her sins and knew the embarrassment she was to society. Her life was worthless to the town and the people. She had very few friends and had to plan ahead to avoid shame just to get a drink of water.

It is easy for us to feel the same way. Either we are not popular enough, or we don't have the high status we think we should. We've messed up too often and realized we cannot return to the good ole days before we fell into

---

[11] GotQuestions.org. (2011, January 17). *Woman at the Well*. https://www.gotquestions.org/woman-at-the-well.html

[12] *Enduring Word Bible Commentary John Chapter 4*. Enduring Word. (2023, April 27). https://enduringword.com/bible-commentary/john-4/

sin. Sin destroys lives and leaves us feeling empty and lonely. The woman at the well is an example of how evil can destroy our character and leave us feeling ashamed and afraid of the perception from others.

If the woman at the well looked at herself in a mirror the morning before she met Jesus, she probably would see nothing but shame and guilt. She knew her life was worthless, but how could she fix it? The acceptance of others would not satisfy her weary soul. Their rejection of her just kept digging the hole of despair in her life. Then she found grace waiting for her at the well. She found forgiveness and the courage to see that she was worth more than she gave herself credit for.

This woman's story continues as we read her response to meeting Jesus, the Messiah. John 4:28-30 (NIV) tells us, "Then, leaving her water jar, the woman went back to the town and said to the people, 'Come, see a man who told me everything I ever did. Could this be the Messiah?' They came out of the town and made their way toward him."

These verses are powerful when you look at the bigger picture of what is happening. This woman left the town in the heat of the day to walk alone to get water from the well. British Bible professor F.F. Bruce said, "If she had avoided the company of her fellow citizens before, she was a changed woman now; she must seek them out and share her news with them."[13]

The woman sought out the same people who looked down on her for her sins and errors to tell them that she had found the Messiah. She wanted others to know the Man who knew everything about her. Finally, she developed the courage to leave everything at the well. She left all her past actions and all the people's opinions of her behind with Jesus at the well and returned to the city a new person. Known beyond her sin, she now discovered a new life in Jesus.

The story of the woman at the well impacts others. Her courage to return home and tell others about meeting Jesus, the Messiah, sparked an interest in the town. The townspeople wanted to learn more. Out of all the people who could have relayed the message of the Messiah's arrival, it was a woman who had been known as a social outcast. Nobody cared for her,

---

[13] *Enduring Word Bible Commentary John Chapter 4*. Enduring Word. (2023, April 27). https://enduringword.com/bible-commentary/john-4/

but now everyone wanted to listen to her. People were attracted to her testimony of a changed life through the grace of Jesus.

The Courage to Be You

A friend once told me never to see my testimony as ordinary. One's testimony is powerful and can lead someone to experience Jesus. The testimony of the woman at the well led others to Jesus. Remember, no one can argue with or tell you your story is wrong.

It took incredible courage for the woman to return to the town where she lived. Her courage was made possible by the powerful words and love of Jesus. When you develop the courage to see that your life has purpose and meaning, you discover the wonders of being used by an Almighty God. Your story is not beyond repair. No sin is too great to keep you from telling others about the level of redemption in your life.

Go look at yourself in the mirror. If Jesus sees potential beyond an outcast like the woman at the well, then He sees the same in you. He notices something more significant in you than you notice in yourself. He sees hope and redemption available for you as He waits for you to come to Him.

Jesus waited patiently for the woman at the well, for He knew she was coming. The woman was unaware the Messiah was waiting for her. You may not realize that Jesus is waiting on you to respond to Him because you are too focused on your mistakes and failures. When you decide to go to the well to talk with Jesus, those mistakes do not matter. What does matter is if you will take a sip of the living water that Jesus has to offer! When you take your eyes off of yourself – and your mistakes or heartaches – and look at Him, you realize that He is all that matters.

Where is your courage found? Is your courage found in the hope of Jesus and how He perceives you? You have more potential than you give yourself credit for. Furthermore, your story matters more than you realize. Take courage today in knowing that when Christ is your Savior, your story is not a mistake. Your identity is not found in your past. Your identity is found in the hopeful glory that is to come in Heaven. Your courage is now found in the redemption God gave you and the story He has entrusted you to share.

Every good story takes time to share. The content of the story matters.

Yes, your past is an important part of your story, but your courage to over-come your sins and see yourself as Christ sees you makes your story power-ful. Now, look at yourself in the mirror and know you have courage and an identity because of Jesus Christ.

Chapter 7
More than My Appearance

My favorite Christmas movie is the 'real people' version of *The Grinch.* I have made it a tradition to watch *The Grinch* at least once during the Christmas season. It is one of the few movies I will never get tired of watching. Some of my friends argue that *National Lampoon's Christmas Vacation* or *Elf* are the greatest Christmas movies, but I disagree.

I love how the Grinch is his own person. Though I obviously don't always agree with his attitudes or the things he says, I admire that he is not afraid to tell the Whos in Whoville how he feels, even if they don't like it. But, spoiler alert, if you have not seen the movie (To which I ask, "Why?!"), the Grinch experiences a change of heart. He changes his character and the way he views the Whos of Whoville and Christmas. At the end of the movie, he happily celebrates Christmas with the entire town of Whoville.

One of the funniest parts in the movie is when Cindy Lou Who tries to investigate the story of the Grinch's childhood. She visits the two ladies who raised the Grinch before he left Whoville to live for several years on the top of Mount Crumpit. Cindy Lou Who is determined to learn more about the Grinch because she thinks he can change. She does not want him to be by himself. Instead, she wants the Grinch to celebrate Christmas with others. The ladies begin to tell Cindy the Grinch's story, starting with how he entered the world.

The scene transitions from Cindy Lou and the two elderly ladies talking about baby Whos flying in baskets over the city of Whoville. The time had come for babies to be delivered to the correct houses. The cool breeze of the winter night in Whoville directed each basket to the place the baby was assigned to, except for one. The wind picked up, causing the basket that baby Grinch was in to collide with another basket. Then, the Grinch's basket got caught in a tree. The ladies that raised the Grinch said he was stuck in the tree all night. The Grinch was mean for most of the movie; however, you cannot help but feel sorry for him after seeing him as a baby, stuck alone in a tree on a cold winter night.

If you have watched The Grinch, you know that the Whos of Whoville are a unique group of people. For starters, they live in a snowflake. They have crazy-looking hair and noses, along with crazy names. The Whos are very different from how God designed His children. Luckily for us, we are created to imitate our Creator. Genesis 1:27 has become increasingly debated, but it is still simple to understand. It says, "So God created mankind in his own image, in the image of God he created them; male and female he created them" (NIV). This concept is very simple and concrete. People in this world are either male or female and are created in God's image.

All of God's people are created uniquely and different from others. You were created by God to be you. Not only that, but God created us with unique features. Writing for *Answers in Genesis*, Joseph Paturi, in his article, "God's Masterpiece," gives a few examples of the uniqueness of humans. He says, "We live in an amazing world. The greatest of all creations is man himself, the marvelous machine – precise and efficient. The human body has a dynamic framework of bone and cartilage called the skeleton. The human skeleton is flexible, with hinges and joints that were made to move." He also says, "We are more than the chemicals that form our body. We are a special creation of God. Man is God's masterpiece – His workmanship, the crown of creation."[14]

Dr. Werner Gritt, author and German engineer, describes a human being by saying, "Without a doubt, the most complex information-processing system in existence is the human body. If we take all human information processes together, i.e., conscious ones (language, information-controlled, deliberate, voluntary movements) and unconscious ones (information-controlled functions of the organs, hormone system), this involves the process-

---

[14] *The Human Body-God's Masterpiece*. Answers in Genesis. (n.d.). https://answersingenesis. org/kids/anatomy/the-human-body/

ing of 1024 bits daily. This astronomically high figure is higher by a factor of 1,000,000 [i.e., is a million times greater] than the total human knowledge of 1018 bits stored in all the world›s libraries.[15]

Statements like these from doctors make you stop and read them twice. Even as I write this chapter, I have had to go back and think about how complex God made us. Yet, I am also reminded of the truth of Psalm 139:14 (NIV), "I praise you because I am fearfully and wonderfully made; your works are wonderful, I know that full well." The human body is unique, but it all points back to a Creator who had our best interest in His mind when He formed us in His image.

Reflecting on my story of being diagnosed with alopecia, I have experienced a new sense of humility. Losing my hair has humbled me enough that I realize I am not in control of what happens to me or how God designed me. God designs His creations with intention. He permits certain things to happen because He knows a greater plan is ahead. God gave you and me unique features. He has created billions of people; each one different from the other. Your genetic code differs from mine, but we share the truth that God created us for His glory. When you realize this truth, you have confidence to look in the mirror, knowing you can embrace yourself because God created you.

How I Embraced Myself

I cannot emphasize enough that embracing my noticeable condition changed how I view myself tremendously. My public image is nothing compared to who I am in God's eyes. My time on earth without hair is nothing compared to how long eternity lasts. So, if God permitted this, there is no changing His plans. My infinite mind cannot understand the plans of a finite God. God has plans for my life. I am to live out these plans according to His time.

Before losing my hair after my ninth birthday, I thought I would look like everyone else. Instead, God knew I would wake up one morning with many pieces of hair on my pillow. He knew I would struggle. God knew

---

[15] *The Human Body-God's Masterpiece - Religion - Nigeria*. Nairaland, the Nigerian Forum. (n.d.). https://www.nairaland.com/7515031/human-bodygods-masterpiece

it would time for me to adjust to my new appearance. Finally, He knew I would be angry with Him. All these changes were a part of a greater plan that I have grown to appreciate watching play out every second of every day.

As years passed, and I matured, I was able to see beyond the emotional pain. I gradually accepted my condition. I stopped questioning God as to why this happened because I realized there was more to my story. There is more to me than this misfortune I live with. There is more to me than alopecia. I, along with others who surrender their lives to Christ, am a vessel used to share God's story. In moments of pride, I remind myself that God can take away anything He has given me without an explanation.

Realizing there is more to my story helped me embrace who I am and the tragedy I experienced when I was nine. The diagnosis of alopecia changed my life, but I eventually knew that my experiences could help someone else. I was also humbled to understand that no one is perfect. Whether someone differs in outer appearance or has an internal struggle, everyone deals with difficult and tiresome circumstances. Unfortunately, the devil attacks everyone and seems to win many battles. The devil easily could have won my battle with struggling to understand God's plan.

I was a prime candidate to give up on my faith. I was angry with God and embarrassed by my new appearance. I tried to hide my hair loss by covering it up. I did not want others to see my bald head because of the fear of being ridiculed. Yes, I did face judgment and jokes, and yes, they hurt. It took looking beyond my physical reflection in the mirror. God helped me understand that alopecia does not define me. My identity is not found in the cruel jokes from others, which easily could have destroyed my confidence.

My identity comes from the fact that I surrendered my life to the One who loves me beyond anything imaginable. My identity is in the One who forgave me even when I did not deserve it. I can embrace myself because God welcomed me with open arms. God sees me as someone He created with a purpose and a vision. He loves me no matter what. Embracing my identity as a "Child of God" helps give me the confidence needed to accept my alopecia. A child of God with a unique condition is a story waiting to be told.

I understand you may struggle to see hope beyond your condition or circumstance. Or you may be living with something you hope no one knows about. Whatever it is, I hope my ability to be real with you helps you see that your identity is not found in your struggles or condition. When you surrender your life to Christ and embrace the life He has for you as His child, a change occurs. You see that you are more than your struggles. You become a new creation (2 Corinthians 5:17) through God. You are His child, and you are His friend.

Being a child of God means you are valuable and precious in your Creator's eyes. You are so valuable to God that He sees beyond your sins and rebellious attitude toward Him, and He died on the cross for you. The Bible says that no one is perfect, and we are all at fault. We have sinned against God (Romans 3:23). Your story is not finished. There is more to come. Your new story starts with a new life in Christ.

Looking at myself in the mirror, knowing that I am a child of God, gave me the confidence to show others what I looked like without hair. I would be remiss if I did not stop right here to encourage you. If you haven't already, embrace God's love and accept the gift of grace available to you. If you have not given your life to Christ, there is no time like the present.

Before reading forward, I ask that you stop and consider where you are in your life right now. Have you indeed given your life to Christ? Are you putting off His tugging at your heart? Are you closing your heart to Him when you should be opening it? If you are ready to accept Christ into your heart and embrace all He has for you, follow what John 1:12 says "Yet to all who did receive him, to those who believed in His name, He gave the right to become children of God."

There are simple steps to take. First, you must receive the gift of grace by acknowledging that grace is not earned. God gives grace through His Son's death on the cross. You must receive forgiveness of your sins by accepting that you have fallen short of the glory of God.

Next, you believe that Jesus is the Son of God, and you believe He died on the cross and rose again on the third day. Then, you ask Him to be the Lord of your life. You surrender to Him fully. God does not want anyone to perish but to have eternal life. (John 3:16).

Once you follow these steps, you become a child of God. God commands you to live out your days proclaiming the Good News by telling others about Him. You should read your Bible, pray to Him, and get baptized. You should join a local church and find a place to serve in your church. God tells His story through you because He has your best interest in mind.

To make things easy, below is an example prayer to God. The purpose of this prayer is to confess your sins, believe in Jesus Christ as Lord, and to become a child of God.

"Dear God, I acknowledge that I am a sinner and have rebelled against you. I have chosen to live a life outside of who you are. I confess my sins to you and ask for your forgiveness. I ask that your Son, Jesus, become Lord of my life. I believe He died on the cross to save me from my sins and rose on the third day. I want to become a child of God. In Jesus's name I pray. Amen."

Suppose you prayed that prayer; I want to be one of the first to welcome you into the family of God. This decision you have made just now is the best decision you will ever make. The decision secures your eternity and allows you to walk in freedom and victory found only in Jesus Christ.

Live Sent

The term "Live Sent" has been on my mind since 2022. These words were placed on my heart as I thought about my favorite Bible verse, Romans 10:15 (NIV), "And how can anyone preach unless they are sent? As it is written: 'How beautiful are the feet of those who bring good news!'"

To truly grasp the importance of being sent by God to share the good news and understand Paul's phrase, "How beautiful are the feet of those who bring good news," you must refer back to a few verses in Romans 10:13-14 (NIV). Paul begins a series of questions by saying, "Everyone who calls on the name of the Lord will be saved. How, then, can they call on the one they have not believed in? And how can they believe in the one whom they have not heard? And how can they hear without someone preaching to them?"

Paul proposed many applicable questions. "Everyone" refers to everyone, whether Greek, Hebrew, Spanish, French, or English. Knowing that my God loves me enough to listen to me when I call on His name is comforting. Paul, who speaks the Word of God, reminds us that it does not matter who we are or from where we come. If we call on the name of the Lord, we will be saved. Now would be a perfect time to look at yourself in the mirror. When you do, you will see someone who has been given an opportunity to call on God's name.

One online commentary, *Bible Ref*, explains it this way, "Now, Paul continues with the next logical question: How will anyone preach the gospel of Jesus unless they are sent by someone to do so? Paul's question shows that preaching is not the first step in the chain that leads to faith in Christ and calling on His name. Instead, sending is that first step. Who does the sending? In the case of Paul and the other apostles preaching the gospel around the world, Christ Himself had sent them out. Jesus had commissioned them to preach the good news to the world."[16]

When I use the term "Live Sent" to describe how I live my life, it reminds me I am not sending myself to proclaim the good news. Neither my parents nor my friends are sending me to proclaim the good news of Jesus. Instead, the power of the Holy Spirit allows me to proclaim the name of Jesus to others. I have failed many times and taken the easy way out. I have been a Jonah and have run in the opposite direction. I have been a Gideon and acted out of fear. I have been a David and felt I had sinned too much to be used by a perfect God.

Yet, I know that I am "living sent" because I can honestly look at myself in the mirror with the revelation that I chose to be defined by God's calling. We should all want to Live Sent for Jesus. We should want to proclaim His name no matter where or what condition we are in. God has given us a field of opportunity and a new audience to reach every day who are desperate to hear the wisdom and truth that they are not defined by their sin. Instead, these individuals have a gift waiting on them. Will you help them receive this gift?

Living sent for Jesus does not mean everyone should be on staff at a

---

[16] *Romans 10:15*. BibleRef.com. (n.d.). https://www.bibleref.com/Romans/10/Romans-10-15.html#:~:text=Now%20Paul%20continues%20with%20the,sending%20is%20that%20first%20step.

church. I am fortunate to have been on staff at a few churches, and I currently run a nonprofit organization called Know Ministries. Know Ministries's mission is that of "providing Bibles to children in the inner cities so that they know Jesus loves them." These opportunities enable me to share the gospel. Look at yourself in the mirror as a Christian. Your first purpose is to follow and obey Jesus. Now, turn around and look at the world of opportunity that awaits you. Get ready and be inspired because your job of sharing the good news with others does not begin tomorrow or next week. It begins now!

Being involved in multiple churches and running Know Ministries have played tremendous roles in knowing my purpose in life. I accepted my call to ministry in 2016 and have enjoyed it since. There have been hard, faithless times. I am confident that these times were not surprising to a faithful God. He has guided me every step of the way.

One way God has guided me is through starting the nonprofit. What makes managing Know Ministries unique is seeing the joy on children's faces when a Bible is placed in their hands. This feeling is heartwarming because a child finds comfort in the Bible. In 2022, I worked alongside a friend and some of his family members in Houston, TX, to minister to lower-income families. Our efforts included caring for the children while their parents waited to get groceries. I will never forget what one of the moms told me.

Although this mom spoke in Spanish, I had someone translate her story to me. At this same time, the war in Ukraine had just begun. This war was frightening to many people, including this mom and her children. However, the mom had an encouraging and inspiring faith that the Bible could comfort her children. She told me and the translator, "My child is afraid of what is happening in the world. Therefore, I wanted him to have a Bible, so hopefully, it would encourage him." That story still warms my heart.

The stories do not stop there. I believe Know Ministries will continue to grow and prosper for years to come. There will be more opportunities to give Bibles and more stories to share. I am humbled when I hear stories of children who live in areas that have little to no access to Bibles. I am grateful to play a role in helping a child receive a Bible for the first time.

I have had many opportunities in many places to provide Bibles to children. Usually, I like to plan Bible distributions in advance. At a minimum, I like to know a month ahead of time when a ministry partner needs Bibles from us. When I do know in advance, I am able to secure volunteers and donors. These individuals can check their schedules to determine how they can help. Whether it is through praying, supporting, writing letters, or something else, I want people to get plugged into how Know Ministries works in a child's life.

However, one time, in 2022, my plans did not work as I thought they would. A few weeks after providing Bibles in Houston, TX, I was back home in Mississippi with another opportunity to give Bibles to children. This next Bible distribution opportunity did not adhere to my time schedule. I was asked to provide a message during a Friday afternoon chapel at a school in Jackson, MS. Not only was I asked to speak, but the school headmaster asked if Know Ministries could provide Bibles to the fifty or more children who would be in attendance. Despite the short notice, I did not turn down this chance to speak to the children.

Thankfully, this opportunity to speak at the school's chapel allowed me to extend an opportunity for a new friend to be a part of what Know Ministries does. I gave the details to her, and we planned to meet at the school to distribute the Bibles to the children. Unfortunately, I did not publicly announce beforehand that we were going to have this Bible distribution happening in Jackson, MS. I wanted to try to enjoy a spur-of-the-moment event. Though I work better when I know and plan in advance, and though planning this Bible distribution with little time was an adjustment, it was worth it.

After meeting my friend in the school parking lot, we discussed the day's events then we walked into the school together to meet the headmaster. This encounter between the headmaster and me sparked much excitement because this was the beginning of a strong ministry partnership and a loyal friendship. This outreach opportunity would be great for the kids of his school. Many of these children were not attending church. At this chapel, the children were able to hear the good news of Jesus Christ.

The headmaster guided us to where we would be for the chapel service and where the children would receive their Bibles. After a few more discussions about the service, I made final preparations for my message while placing Bibles where they needed to be. As the students began to fill the room, the chapel service began. It was now time for me to speak.

My devotional went well. I discussed what makes a good story and tied it into how the Bible is the best story they will ever read. I spoke on this topic so that when the students received a Bible they would be genuinely interested to read about Jesus. After talking about how the Bible is the best story anyone will read, I was glad that the students were excited to receive their new Bibles.

My friend who volunteered with me that day made sure that every child present received a Bible. I was glad that she got to experience how much joy comes from placing a Bible in a child's hand. As I look at pictures from this day, I am reminded that sometimes the best opportunities to share the Gospel with others are not planned. That truth was revealed after the headmaster, my friend, and I heard a student say something we would never forget.

That student approached us, and said, "This is my first Bible." I was distracted a little at that time and did not clearly hear what she said. However, the headmaster did and asked me if I had heard what the student said. When he explained what the student said, I could not believe what he told me. This student was so excited to receive her first Bible! I was glad to be able to share this moment with her.

To this day, I still have the picture of the student, my friend, and I together. This picture makes me smile because stories like the one from this student remind me of the importance of embracing what God has for you. You never know what God will do or who He will use to make a difference in your life. He has invited us to embrace our callings as He reveals more pieces of our story as we journey with Him. The student's grateful and joyful smile encourages me that the Bible can tremendously impact a child's life for eternity.

My journey into ministry helped me discover that I enjoy what God has called me to do. Stories like a child receiving her first Bible or a mother wanting her son to find comfort in the Bible remind me that there is a world of people who need God's truth. These stories are part of why I started Know Ministries. I will continue striving to follow God's plan with this ministry.

I have had wonderful experiences in ministry and know there are more to come. I humbly admit that I must always remember not to let pride keep me from seeing what God is doing. Letting my pride get in the way of the work God has called me to do could lead me to miss God's blessings. I must focus on Him rather than building myself up. Thankfully, God has used situations in my life to lessen my pride and embrace what He has in store. That's right, I can be thankful even for my alopecia.

Chapter 8
The Road Ahead

I surrendered to the call of ministry in the fall semester of my senior year of high school in 2016. Funnily enough, the decision happened in a process that led me to discover God's a sense of humor. A friend once told me, "If you want to make God laugh, tell Him your plans." Psalm 139:4 says, "Before a word is on my tongue you, Lord, know it completely."

Before I spoke my plans to God, He knew what I would say. He knew that I would spend the summer of 2016, before my senior year of high school, waking up each day so I could find my mom and tell her my new decision on my future career path. God knew I would tell my mom, "Here is the new career I want to choose." I planned to be a psychologist, own a business, or become a politician. Three different occupations, but I was determined to do something special. I was determined to make a name for myself. I was chasing my dreams.

I was finding my identity in myself. Little did I know that while discovering that God was calling me into ministry, I was also falling victim to the dangers of pride. I often hide this struggle and try to present myself as humble. Yet sometimes I wonder if people see me as cocky and prideful or if people know that I was just kidding when saying I was the best at something.

I felt the closer I got into ministry, the more I was becoming too proud of my progress. This attitude and way of thinking became apparent when I formed Know Ministries in 2016 during my senior year of high school. I jokingly enjoy the memory of sitting in a certified public account's office in Meridian, MS, with a piece of paper in front of me waiting for my signature on a line with the words "Bishop Barlow, CEO" below. Still, to this day, people laugh at me for being seventeen years old and having the titles "President and CEO" behind my name. I tend to go along with their jokes, but I also fall victim to finding my identity in titles.

My struggle with finding my identity in pride and titles grew as I made prominent connections in the ministry world. Do I know every famous pastor, youth pastor, or ministry leader? No, I do not, but it has been enjoyable breaking out of my shyness, meeting new people, and building lasting friendships in ministry. For three and a half years, I loved seeing the busyness of my calendar on my phone. I loved having days going from one meeting to the next. I also loved planning events and pretending I could survive on a minimum amount of sleep.

Little did I know that I was beginning to miss vital opportunities to grow Know Ministries. I thought it took multiple meetings a week to build an organization. However, I failed to realize that I needed to invest in the structure and internal growth of the organization and the public side. I cherish any time I meet with my ministry friends because most of them have invested so much time in teaching me what they have learned since they were my age. But, more and more, I felt myself wearing thin as I continued to add meetings to my calendar. I found my identity by saying, "Look at how busy I am and who I get to meet with today."

In January 2020, Know Ministries celebrated providing over 1,000 children with personal Bibles. We had a night of celebration that I wanted to go all out for, with hopes of impressing many people. I put in lots of work for that event. This paid off as many people approached me, praising me for a well-done job. These were thoughtful and kind comments from lots of my friends, but I let it build my pride up further.

I thought we were invincible, and Know Ministries was about to make it big. I thought this night of celebration would be the moment that launched the organization from "That is Bishop's Nonprofit," to "Wow, Know Ministries has grown so much that people across the world know who we are!" My pride continued to build, and my plans continued to be all about how big I could make my name.

A month after our night of celebration, I held Know Ministries' annual board meeting. I asked those in attendance about my vision to see Know

Ministries use this accomplishment to show potential significant donors that we are doing great things and ask them to join us in what God is doing in the inner cities through us. The board agreed that we could begin having those conversations, but then everything began to change.

A few weeks after our board meeting, I was driving home from a meeting with a new ministry partner in New Orleans, LA. At this time, I began to hear rumors that the world was changing due to a virus spreading across the globe at a record pace. Before this meeting, I paid little attention and was not worried. Instead, I laughed while watching sporting events get canceled. I did enjoy knowing that my college extended our spring break!

I felt something was wrong on that drive home to Mississippi from New Orleans. The news and confusion from the world were unlike anything I'd ever heard of in my lifetime. I tried not to let it phase me and make me panic, especially since Know Ministries was about to have another major Bible distribution event a month after my meeting in New Orleans. On my drive home, a ministry partner texted me, "Don't you dare cancel the event." "Of course not," I thought.

The confusion and panic from the world grew, and events I was sure would not be canceled changed their plans. The news kept coming in that the virus we now know as the coronavirus, or Covid-19, was spreading quickly, and leaders worldwide were instituting drastic safety measures and locking the world down. Schools were to go remote for the remainder of the semester, businesses shut down, and live sporting events were nonexistent. Due to restrictions at the time, I had no choice but to postpone our ministry plans to work with multiple churches around Mississippi to distribute Bibles to children. I could not listen to the advice from my ministry partner to have my next big event, even though I wanted to.

Not only did I have to announce the decision to postpone Know Ministries' April 2020 Bible distribution event, but I also had to delete meetings I scheduled on my calendar. I will never forget how my February 2020 calendar compared to my March 2020 calendar: full to empty. During the last two weeks of February 2020, I had multiple meetings each day. As I swipe over to March 2020, it is massively different, containing very few events. Sometimes I wanted to put "Walmart trip" on my March 2020 calendar to make it seem like I had plans.

My world changed (just like it did for everyone else). Nobody really knew what to do, and everyone tried to form opinions on when things might go back to normal. Everything that I found my identity in was on pause. No Bibles were distributed to children, and no meetings were held. I had little to post about on social media because we were not doing anything significant for a while. When I looked in the mirror at myself, I knew I had to do something different, or I would go crazy.

Realizing There Is More Than a Calendar

There was no special moment in lockdown that I realized that Know Ministries was a mess internally. But I remember increasingly thinking that something needed to change, and now I had all the time in the world to work on organizing the structure of the ministry. We needed strategies in place and a stronger *why* behind our mission statement. We needed firm plans on how we would distribute Bibles to children. Then, humbled, I admitted that Know Ministries was not ready to take a business or strategy plan to a potential major investor and ask for support.

I dreamed of receiving millions of dollars for Know Ministries, all the while neglecting to recognize the impact $5 can make. My pride got in the way of seeing God's blessings. I let my desire to make my name great get in the way of making God's name known. Thankfully, at the same time I was thinking things were not looking good for Know Ministries, God showed me it was an opportunity for growth for the organization. Surprisingly, we began to have our best financial years yet. Most importantly, it was when God started to break me of dreams and goals I thought I wanted.

When I began Know Ministries in 2016, I told myself that this organization would be my job by the time I graduated college. I wanted to be like other young nonprofit entrepreneurs who had national organizations in their twenties. So, I did what I could to grow Know Ministries while taking college courses. I tried to enjoy building friendships while creating and managing events. Sometimes I wonder if I neglected moments for the sake of scheduling newsletters. I wonder if I should have gone with my friends to hang out at a coffee shop on campus rather than edit a website page. It felt good at the moment, but was it my pride?

I admit to you that my dream did not come true. Know Ministries did not become my full-time job after I walked across the stage to receive my college diploma. God had other plans, and those plans included more schooling. Since answering "yes" to ministry, I felt that God was leading me to attend seminary. I knew I would continue my education after college and pursue my master's degree. I wanted to work more on Know Ministries, but God had a different idea. He put people in my life who told me, "People respect people with education," and "You need to continue your education before anything else."

I knew that was wise advice but did not want to listen. While looking in the mirror, I saw someone determined to listen to myself instead of what God was trying to speak to me through others. The old saying, "That went in one ear and out the other" applied to me when people told me to finish my education. But my dreams and goals did not come true as Know Ministries was not my full-time job when I graduated college.

Did I fail? The answer depends on who you ask. Hindsight is 20/20, and knowing what I know now and having been through the unique opportunities God has opened since I embraced the call of ministry, I would not trade it for the world. It always amazes me that whenever we let God's plans unfold and stop trying to force our own, we always return to God saying, "You were right." Even when we do not know what He is doing, God never fails in His promises.

Sometimes I feel I can stare in the mirror and look back at myself, knowing I had two roads before me when I graduated from Mississippi College in 2021. There I stood with two open roads that never ended; the two roads had signs in front of them. One roadside sign read, "My way." The caption below read, "Follow this road and do what you want. You deserve it." It was tempting.

The second sign read, "God's way." No caption necessary. No plans were revealed. Both signs seemed promising, but only one led to a glorious end.

It is easy to find our identities in status or in how successful we are. Finding your identity in God's plans takes longer than finding your identity in yourself. Shouldn't we live by the motto, "If you want it done right, you should do it yourself."? Why did I need to follow God's way? Why do you need to follow God's way? The more days go by on this earth, the more I see us gravitating towards an all-about-me attitude. The danger in that mindset is missing that our identity is in the One who made us, and the One who made us did so with good intentions for His good purpose.

I answered the call to ministry in 2016, and for years I thought I wanted to be a pastor. The problem was I tended to close my mind to any other job in ministry. If I was not going to be the man in charge, then I did not want to do it. To this day, I do not enjoy working for people because I want to be in charge. Again, my pride almost kept me from seeing God's plan. I was so prideful that I joked that I knew more than God's plan for my life. One of the careers I had no desire for was youth minister or child's minister. Ironic, yes?

I loved telling stories about how Know Ministries has made a difference in the lives of thousands of children in the inner cities, but I had no desire to work in a church as a youth minister. I was not doing Know Ministries or seminary because I wanted to be a senior pastor, but that is what I planned to do when thinking about seminary classes. Since answering yes to ministry in 2016, I spoke, for the next five years, about becoming a church's senior pastor.

In the summer of 2021, everything changed.

A Change in the Journey

The last few chapters of the book of Genesis tell the story of Joseph. Most of the story speaks of his time in Egypt after his brothers sold him into slavery. However, Joseph was a jerk to his brothers before that took place. They could not stand him. He was so arrogant and prideful. Genesis 37:3-11 explains:

> *3 Now Israel loved Joseph more than any of his other sons, because he had been born to him in his old age; and he made an ornate robe for him. 4 When his brothers saw that their father loved him more than any of them, they hated him and could not speak a kind word to him. 5 Joseph had a dream, and when he told it to his brothers, they hated him all the more. 6 He said to them, "Listen to this dream I had: 7 We were binding sheaves of grain out in the field when suddenly my sheaf rose and stood upright, while your sheaves gathered around mine and*

bowed down to it."

8 His brothers said to him, "Do you intend to reign over us? Will you actually rule us?" And they hated him all the more because of his dream and what he had said.

9 Then he had another dream, and he told it to his brothers. "Listen," he said, "I had another dream, and this time the sun and moon and eleven stars were bowing down to me."

10 When he told his father as well as his brothers, his father rebuked him and said, "What is this dream you had? Will your mother and I and your brothers actually come and bow down to the ground before you?" 11 His brothers were jealous of him, but his father kept the matter in mind.

I never wanted people to see me as prideful or arrogant. People affirmed that I had great leadership qualities and could be a senior pastor one day. I denied any thought of another calling into ministry other than being the senior pastor of a church and being the president of Know Ministries. Perhaps Joseph was not trying to be arrogant to his brothers, but he made them mad to the point that they sold him into slavery because they did not want to see him again. I learned that my attitude could have been arrogance against God's plans, and I could have been trying to put myself on a pedestal I was not intended to be on. God began to work in me to open my heart to humility and submission, not prideful close-mindedness.

In the summer of 2021, a youth ministry friend asked me to be an adult chaperone on a youth trip to a Florida beach. I laughed because I spent most of that summer volunteering with the same youth group and acting like a child most of the time. This part of my story is ironic because I have been building it up as one where I did not want to be in youth ministry, and now I am enjoying it. It was a great summer with the youth, and everything was building towards one moment on that trip to the beach.

On one of the last nights of the youth trip, I stood on the pier that led to the beach. I stood alone in one of the few moments I had to myself on that trip. It felt like no one was around, and it was just me staring, not into a mirror, but the endless amount of black in the sky. The waves continued peacefully crashing into the shore. A nice cool breeze continually blew. There I was, just me and an endless sky.

This time, I did not have two roads in front of me, and I was not forced to choose between two paths. Instead, I found myself staring in one direction. I did not have a choice this time. I felt as if my life was leading to only one place at that time, and it was the place I'd refused to accept for five years. Was God leading me to youth ministry?

I write this last chapter not knowing where I will be in twenty years. Maybe one day, I will be a senior pastor. But, like Joseph going into an unknown area, I realized that what is not known to me is known to God. It just takes time for me to see it. Joseph did not know how his story would end. He did not realize that God would make good out of evil. (Genesis 50:20) He did what he could to trust in God. I continue to try to do the same thing.

Life can be hard sometimes because we do not know the end. We do not know what the future is for our lives, so we like to dream and pretend. We want to imagine that one day all our dreams will come true, but the reality is that what we desire is nothing compared to what God laid out before the earth's foundations were formed. We stare at ourselves in the mirror with determination to achieve our goals, looking past the pride that keeps us from seeing that God has something better.

That night in Florida, as I stared into the night sky, I felt a weight come off me. It was all the pride and resistance to God beginning to leave me. I thought I was missing something, and it was becoming clear that God had plans I did not see until now. I left that pier saying, "Okay, God, you are doing something. I do not know what it is, but you are doing something, and I'm ready to join in whatever you have for me."

I asked earlier, "Was God calling me to youth ministry?" I began to explore the possibilities of that calling when I returned home from that church beach trip. I began to ask trusted adults in my life what they thought, and the same ones that felt I could be a senior pastor one day also affirmed that I had what it took to be a youth minister. Some even believed I should pursue that calling more than that of a senior pastor. They also assured me that pursuing a career in youth ministry does not mean I cannot be a senior pastor one day.

My attitude towards my life and goals began to change. I felt things change so much that I began to appreciate my ministry more, and seeing how each child receives a Bible has helped me see the joy in God's Word. Joseph did not know what would happen to him each day he was in Egyptian bondage. Still, the more he trusted God and let go of his arrogant ways, the more he saw God was using his brother's awful decision to sell him into slavery to save the country of Israel. God does the same in our lives as he takes the good or bad we face and uses it as part of the story He tells on Earth.

In August 2021, I entered my first classes of seminary. I felt confident I was going in the right direction. I was no longer trying to decide what road to follow or take. The decision was made as I accepted God's path. Thankfully I obeyed because I felt God open doors that have led me to where I am today. Do I struggle with pride and arrogance still? Yes, but it has become easier to remain in submission to God's will and denial of myself as I have noticed that there is peace when walking down God's path. The path is smooth, whereas my way would have led to rocky roads. Do I sometimes fall on the smooth soil of God's path? Yes, but I know I have a Savior who picks me up and continues to walk with me.

God is like that. You will fall at certain times when you are on His path and doing His will. We sin and stray from God. We sometimes try to leave our walk with God and return to our rocky path. We might even achieve the goal of leaving God to return to our path. But there is beauty in forgiveness and finding our identity in God's grace. We may walk for a while on God's path and then return to the dangers of our own.

You know you are on God's path when you have peace about where you are, which is unexplainable to everyone else. You rest easy, and you enjoy your days. You want to get up because of the sheer excitement that you are attending a class or job you enjoy. Look in the mirror, and know your identity is that of a child of God living His calling for your life. The reflection looking back at you is a person living in peace, no longer trying to fit personal plans into God's plans. The person looking back at you in the mirror is no longer trying to be God and take control of the things only the God outside of time can control. In August 2021, I felt this peace. But even when I felt this peace, my struggle with pride was still there, and I still desired for some of my plans to hurry up.

Learn to Enjoy the Story God is telling through You

When we grow closer to God and live for Him, the devil's attacks on our flesh begin to remind us of the comfortable side of life. The devil loves to take us on a detour when we are on God's path. The difference in this detour is he tries to trick us by hoping we will never realize that his path never leads us back to God.

Our flesh does the same thing – the Bible tells us we are naturally in rebellion with God's plan. Ever since sin was introduced in the Garden of Eden, we are born into the sinful bloodline, and we desire the things of the world instead of Heavenly things. Paul tells the Colossians in his letter, "Set your minds on things above, not on earthly things." (Colossians 3:2) This is hard for us because we were born into sin. We were born not appreciating the love of God.

It was only a matter of time until the desire to find my identity in having a well-known name and image in ministry returned. Unfortunately, I also desired to rush God's story instead of finding peace in enjoying the ride. This mindset was especially true when it came to Know Ministries. As we returned to in-person Bible distribution events after pausing many plans in 2020, I had moments where I doubted that God was faithful to the work we were doing. It sounds crazy to think that God would not be devoted to providing children a copy of His Word, but I had moments where I doubted more than enjoying the story God was telling.

I can tell plenty of examples, but one of the most prominent examples of my lack of faith was in October 2022 in Jackson, MS. The plans for a big event in Jackson, MS (Know Ministries' home city), began to take place in early summer 2022. I can recall talking with different ministry partners and the board of directors about my vision for another major event. Everyone agreed to the plan, and things moved forward.

On June 20, 2022, I announced on Know Ministries' social media that we planned to host an event called The Light 2022 at a park in Jackson, MS. The Light 2022 would be different from anything we had done in the past because this time we were inviting churches and organizations in the area to take control and plan fun games and activities for the children. They were also encouraged to distribute flyers and other materials about their churches and organizations so children and families could follow up with them.

This time, I had months to plan this event. I am thankful that I did because, while planning this event, I also had a summer internship at a church in Mississippi and was interviewing for another one in Texas. I did what I could to plan The Light 2022 and worked with others who helped me along the way. Thankfully, I had people who were faithful to Know Ministries who helped make everything happen. The park was ready. But, I was not.

I woke up on the morning of The Light 2022 with doubt. Something did not feel right; I believe it was a case of little faith. I could hear Jesus's words to Peter when He said, "You have little faith" (Matthew 8:26, NIV). I could not let others see that I had little faith of the event being successful. I did my best to hide my doubt and feelings of dread.

My feelings still were not improving as I watched the churches and organizations that volunteered to help arrive. My mom jokingly tells me sometimes, "You've got to put on your happy face." This time, it was true. I had to smile and act like everything was going great, instead of telling others that I did not think any children would show up. I did everything I could to have children show up. I supplied other ministries with enough materials to invite children and families to the event. They knocked on doors in the neighborhood around the park the week before and invited lots of children and families. I felt confident in their report that lots of people were interested. Unfortunately, that confidence left me the morning of The Light 2022 and was nowhere to be found when I looked at my watch. It was time to start the event, and there were no kids there yet.

I had to adjust the schedule and ask all volunteers to leave the park and invite the community around the park to our event. I stayed behind only to keep getting reports such as, "There are no children," and "No one is answering the doors." Nothing was working, and my faith was leaving. I was beginning to prepare to cancel the event, something I have never done. I was preparing for the embarrassment of letting every follower on social media know that the event we had promoted for months had gone wrong.

A friend of mine that day tried to remind me that we can still glorify God. It was a truth I did not want to hear at that time. I appreciated the kindness, but it did little to increase my faith at that time. Another volunteer even noticed that I had a look of failure on my face. I was preparing to announce that it was time to pack up and go home. I was about to open my mouth to make the announcement when I saw a young boy and his uncle.

I was talking with my friend, who was trying to encourage me, when I saw this child and his uncle. I told my friend we should meet this child and invite him to The Light 2022. We walked over to the child and his uncle and invited them to enjoy the balloon animals, face painting, giveaways, cookies, and Bibles at our event. I wish you could have seen the excitement on the little boy's face when we told him about all the activities!

I wish you could have been there in person when this little boy ran around and visited every church and organization that volunteered to host a tent and plan an activity for The Light 2022. He was so happy, and we all embraced him. We welcomed him with open arms and did our best to enjoy our time with him and his uncle. The best part was watching his excitement for the balloon animals we gave him.

As I watched this young boy have one of the best days of his life, I noticed more children and families begin to walk up. It seemed like they showed up in droves. I was excited to see people attend. My volunteers worked hard, and now it was beginning to pay off. My lack of faith diminished and turned into a punch of reality. It was almost like I heard God shout, "Have faith in my plans!"

I went back to my friend, who tried to encourage me. I told him he was right, and he reminded me of a truth I will never forget. He said, "God wants us to bring our seed and watch as He grows the garden." We need to be faithful with the little we have and let God take control of everything else.

I will never forget the lessons I learned from The Light 2022. They are lessons I want to leave you with. Look in the mirror again, and remind yourself that you only need to offer what little you have to God. Do not rush the story He wants to tell through you. Everyone has a story and those who are living their lives for God and finding their identities in how God sees them know that they are a part of the greatest story anyone will ever hear.

Enjoy who you are, and embrace what God has planned for you. Others do not define you, no matter how you look or act. Do not change for anyone else. Give your pain to God instead of letting it destroy your confidence in His faithfulness. Accept that you are unique and have a story to tell. Have the courage to be who you are, and enjoy the blessing of life God has given you. Look in the mirror and realize God created you for a reason with a story to tell. Bring your seed to God and watch as He grows a garden. Watch as God uses that seed to produce a beautiful garden. That beautiful garden is staring back at you when you take the time to look in the mirror.

Conclusion

Thank you for walking with me through the trauma of going bald at nine years old. Because what I experienced was so emotionally disturbing, I am better able to bond with and understand others when they go through traumatic events of their own. Alan Loving, a trusted mentor and influence in my ministry, is one such friend.

I met Alan Loving in 2019 when he was the youth pastor at First Baptist Church of Madison, MS, and I was a sophomore at Mississippi College, trying to find my next step in life. I had already accepted the call to ministry and thought I was destined to be a senior pastor. During my sophomore year, my family and I attended Loving's church. I remember my mom telling me that the church hired lots of Mississippi College students to intern in the youth ministry. Without hesitation, I asked my mom if she had Alan Loving's phone number. Thankfully, she did, and she gladly passed it along to me.

As soon as I received Alan's contact, I sent him an email. I felt confident I would hear something back. However, the more I checked my email inbox, the more disappointed I became because Alan had not responded to my email about potentially interning with the youth ministry. After a few days, I mustered up the courage to call Alan. He answered, but his response was discouraging.

"Unfortunately, Bishop, we do not have any open spots in our internship program right now." "Great," I thought to myself, sarcastically. My mom had given me false hope. I tried to sound like I was not disappointed, but I was. I wanted to be an intern so I could have some start in church ministry. But, as our conversation continued, Alan said something that made me hopeful. He continued, "But, if you ever want to come volunteer with us, I will never turn that down." Without hesitation, I agreed.

After a year of volunteering with Alan and the youth at First Baptist Madison, I graduated from Mississippi College and moved to Fort Worth, TX to begin seminary at Southwestern Baptist Theological Seminary in August 2021. Near the end of my first semester of seminary, I received a text message from Alan one Saturday night in April 2022. He said, "Hey bro, would you want to intern with us this summer?" Again, without hesitation, I agreed.

I was Alan's summer intern from May 2022 to August 2022 before I moved back to Texas to begin another church internship. To say that I had a great time with Alan and his team that summer would be an understatement. It was one of my favorite summers I have ever had. I learned that youth ministry means you do not get to take many summer vacations because you need to be with the youth you are serving. But Alan made serving fun, and the opportunity to learn from him is one I will cherish forever.

Before I conclude this book, I want to honor my friend. His story of overcoming a difficulty and trusting in God always encourages me. His faith and reliance on God to get him through reminds me that I can have the same faith in God. I also include Alan's story because I know he, too, would look in the mirror and look past his physical condition and see it as an opportunity to share how God is faithful to him. Did God heal him? No. Did God use Alan to remind others that He is faithful? Yes. Read on to experience Alan's incredible story of struggle and faith in his own words.

Alan Loving's Story

In the 2008 movie *Slumdog Millionaire*, an 18-year-old Jamal Malik of India sweats under the spotlight and pressure of being a contestant on *Who Wants to Be a Millionaire*. This movie portrays that, if we pay attention, our life's journey can provide us with knowledge of how to succeed in life. In the movie, Jamal is able to answer the questions that are posed to him because of a myriad of mostly painful events that occurred in his life. He embraced the concept of not wasting trauma.

I identify with Jamal in learning from and making our trauma benefit us, no matter how unexpected or harsh it may seem. The two verses on the first page of this book illustrate to me how we are to learn from yesterday in order to make tomorrow better, and to try and make every moment count. I have had an amazing life, and I truly feel that I am the most blessed man alive. Some may wonder how I can say such things.

Before we back up too far, I have to paint you a picture of what led to me to leave my career after more than two decades of moving around Mississippi in different Baptist pastoral roles, graduating with both undergraduate (Mississippi College) and graduate (New Orleans Baptist Theological Seminary) degrees, and welcoming two daughters into my family. My wife Courtney and our daughters Mary Addison and Anna Claire have moved time and again with me so we could share the gospel. My entire career has been serving the local church, and I am so grateful that I have been allowed that honor. In March of 2023, I left. Let me back up a bit.

On October 12, 2022, everything changed. I went to my parents' house in Brandon, MS to blow off leaves and pine straw from their roof. I don't remember the fall. I apparently lost my balance and fell on my head on their concrete driveway and sustained a debilitating, complete injury to the T4 vertebrae of my spine. I went from being an active, healthy 51-year-old athletic male to basically being confined to a hospital bed for the next six months... and then realizing that I would never walk again.

I coded three times at the University of Mississippi Medical Center (UMMC) in Jackson, MS. The prayers my family and friends lifted on my behalf, and the brilliant doctors there, kept me alive. I was intubated, given a *tracheotomy, a neck collar, hooked up to a ventilator, given a colostomy, and a foley bag (for urine secretion). The doctors and nurses at UMMC were amazing, and I will be forever grateful for how they took care of me. I do not remember anything from my time there. I left UMMC and went to Select Specialties, a critical illness recovery hospital in Jackson, MS, for five weeks.*

While I was at Select, I got off the ventilator, began to eat solid foods, removed the neck brace, and finally got my tracheotomy removed. Unfortunately, due to never getting turned while at Select, I developed a massive, deep bedsore. I left Select and was given the amazing opportunity to go to The Shepherd Center in Atlanta. Everything about Shepherd was fantastic! Every doctor, nurse, desk attendant, PRN, PT, OT, assistant, cafeteria worker, and custodian – literally anyone we encountered – was superb. I was there 14 weeks because I had to have my bed sore operated on and then was on strict bed rest for four weeks.

While at Shepherd I received a power chair that I was able to leave with when the hospital flew us home. Shepherd prepared us for life when we were able to come home and equipped us for the myriad of changes that we would face upon arrival at our home in Madison, MS.

While at Shepherd it was often commented to me that I had a great attitude and a good disposition. When people would ask how I could be so positive, I would explain that this is only a part of my journey, and that I could face it with a smile knowing I'm one of the luckiest men alive because of my faith, family, and friends. That statement is not only true now but is also true of my entire life and the triad of support that has shaped me.

I can tell you I'm a blessed man because, while there are all kinds of families, the unconditional love and support of mine has been incredible to me. My parents love the Lord; this was their foundation for raising my brother, Matthew Loving, and me. They raised us to marry well and raise our kids as they did us.

My wife and my two girls have cried, laughed, tolerated, supported, encouraged, and helped me. My three girls mean everything to me! I would do anything for them, and I'm pretty sure they feel the same. When I look around, I see families that do not have even close to the amount of support that I have, and I am unbelievably grateful!

I have incredible friends who have prayed for and with me. I have friends who have spoken truth into my life and supplied me with great advice. Proverbs 13:20 reads, "If you walk with the wise, you grow wise; but a companion of fools suffers harm." Since I was young, I've had friends who are wise, who are also a part of the "great crowd of witnesses," cheering me on towards Christ as mentioned in Hebrews 12:1. Literally, if I were to list by name all the people who have influenced, instructed, and shaped me this would become a Faulkner novel.

My faith is what keeps my perspective of life constant. It's what gives me the joy that keeps my spirits up and forms me into the natural encourager I was made to be. Faith is something that people tend to argue about. I became a Christian at an early age, and my relationship with Christ is something that has fueled me, kept me going when life was unbelievably tough, and is something I could never deny. His salvation is one that I have been working out my entire life.

Winston Churchill said, "All men make mistakes, but only the wise learn from them". You might call me crazy when I say that my difficulties have been blessings in my life. I have to remember that divine difficulties are providential. Divine Difficulties aren't disappointments, but they are discipline for your development. I say this as one who was told I'd never run with my daughters, walk with my wife, or be able to play tennis again.

I started this book with Proverbs 3:5-6 and I Corinthians 10:31 because these verses encompass divine difficulties. These verses have helped me to develop my two mantras for life:

Investment is Greater Than Accomplishment (I>A).

The first step in being a hero in someone's life is showing up.

For better or worse, we are all products of the investments of others in us. We've seen the harm done when that investment is abandonment, rejection, or abuse. We must be those are showing up to invest in others in positive, simple ways. Those investments lead to accomplishments. God used the divine difficulties in my life to show me opportunities to help others.

While Alan and I had different traumatic events happen to us, I find two similarities in our conditions. First, God may not heal or give you what you want. We have to look in the mirror and be confident in who we are, children of God. Second, God is always faithful. No matter if God heals us or not, God will always be with us.

My hope is you have finished reading this book with a new confidence and can look in the mirror and see that you are a beloved child of God. You were created by God with a purpose. After you accept this identity, turn from the mirror and leave with confidence that God is with you.

Sources

Enduring Word Bible Commentary John Chapter 4. Enduring Word. (2023, April 27). https://enduringword.com/bible-commentary/john-4/

GotQuestions.org. (2022, August 17). *Truly this was the Son of God.* https://www.gotquestions.org/truly-this-was-the-Son-of-God.html

GotQuestions.org. (2011, January 17). *Woman at the Well.* https://www.gotquestions.org/woman-at-the-well.html

MacArthur, John. "Job," In *The MacArthur Bible Commentary.* edited by John MacArthur, 1,156. Nashville, TN.: Thomas Nelson, 2005.

MacArthur, John. "Matthew," In *The MacArthur Bible Commentary.* edited by John MacArthur, 593. Nashville, TN.: Thomas Nelson, 2005.

Merriam-Webster. (n.d.). *Wake-up call definition & meaning.* Merriam-Webster. https://www.merriam-webster.com/dictionary/wake-up%20call

Romans 10:15. BibleRef.com. (n.d.). https://www.bibleref.com/Romans/10/Romans-10-15.html#:~:text=Now%20Paul%20continues%20with%20the,sending%20is%20that%20first%20step.

Shmoop Editorial Team. (2008b, November 11). *Quotes - Mirror, mirror on the wall, who is the fairest of them all?.* Shmoop. https://www.shmoop.com/quotes/mirror-mirror-on-the-wall.html

Shmoop Editorial Team. (2008a, November 11). *Quotes - because it is my name!.* Shmoop. https://www.shmoop.com/quotes/because-it-is-my-name.html

The Human Body-God's Masterpiece. Answers in Genesis. (n.d.). https://answersingenesis.org/kids/anatomy/the-human-body/

The Human Body-God's Masterpiece - Religion - Nigeria. Nairaland, the Nigerian Forum. (n.d.). https://www.nairaland.com/7515031/human-bodygods-masterpiece

Tomhasker. (2023, February 5). *How Thomas Edison's mother was the making of him...* Lighthouse Community. https://www.lighthousecommunity. global/post/how-thomas-edison-s-mother-was-the-making-of-him

U.S. Department of Health and Human Services. (2024, September 6). *Alopecia areata.* National Institute of Arthritis and Musculoskeletal and Skin Diseases. https://www.niams.nih.gov/health-topics/alopecia-areata

Wellman, P. J. (2015, December 8). *42 quotes about anger.* ChristianQuotes. info. https://www.christianquotes.info/quotes-by-topic/quotes-about-anger/

Made in the USA
Columbia, SC
07 January 2025

51336471R00074